★ ★

Building Projects for
BACKYARD FARMERS
AND HOME GARDENERS

★ ★

★ ★

Building Projects for
BACKYARD FARMERS
AND HOME GARDENERS

★ ★

A Guide to 21 Handmade Structures
for Homegrown Harvests

Chris Gleason

Fox Chapel
PUBLISHING

© 2012 by Chris Gleason and Fox Chapel Publishing Company, Inc..

Building Projects for Backyard Farmers and Home Gardeners is an original work, first published in 2012 by Fox Chapel Publishing Company, Inc. The patterns contained herein are copyrighted by the author. Readers may make copies of these patterns for personal use. The patterns themselves, however, are not to be duplicated for resale or distribution under any circumstances. Any such copying is a violation of copyright law. Published and distributed in North America by Fox Chapel Publishing Company, Inc., East Petersburg, PA.

ISBN 978-1-56523-543-4

Publisher's Cataloging-in-Publication Data

Gleason, Chris, 1973-

    Building projects for backyard farmers and home gardeners : a guide to 21 handmade structures for homegrown harvests / Chris Gleason. -- 1st ed. -- East Petersburg, PA : Fox Chapel Publishing, c2012.

    p. ; cm.

    ISBN: 978-1-56523-543-4
    Includes index.
    Summary: Photo-illustrated step-by-step instructions to show how to build gardening structures. Includes helpful tips and profiles of several backyard farmers.

    1. Garden structures--Design and construction--Amateurs' manuals. 2. Greenhouses--Design and construction--Amateurs' manuals. 3. Cold frames--Design and construction--Amateurs' manuals. 4. Vegetable gardening--Equipment and supplies. 5. Kitchen gardens--Equipment and supplies. 6. Rabbit hutches--Design and construction--Amateurs' manuals. 7. Beehives--Design and construction--Amateurs' manuals. I. Title.

TH4961 .G54 2012
690/.892--dc23   2012

To learn more about the other great books from Fox Chapel Publishing, or to find a retailer near you, call toll-free 800-457-9112 or visit us at *www.FoxChapelPublishing.com*.

Note to Authors: We are always looking for talented authors to write new books in our area of woodworking, design, and related crafts. Please send a brief letter describing your idea to Acquisition Editor, 1970 Broad Street, East Petersburg, PA 17520.

Printed in China
First printing

About the Author

Chris Gleason is the author of several books for the DIY market including *Art of the Chicken Coop, Built-In Furniture for the Home, The Complete Kitchen Makeover, Complete Custom Closet, Old-School Workshop Accessories,* and *Building Real Furniture for Everyday Life*. He grew up on a farm in upstate New York. He has been raising chickens in his Salt Lake City backyard for over six years. He currently builds and sells chicken coops. He has owned Gleason Woodworking Studios for over 13 years.

CONTENTS

ABOUT BACKYARD FARMING

An old proverb reminds us that there is nothing new under the sun, and in the case of the backyard farm, that is certainly true. And while it is exciting to see that small-scale food production is enjoying a notable resurgence in popularity, it is hardly a brand new concept.

Unfortunately, however, modern farming techniques, political policies, and economies of scale have combined to create a culture where growing one's own food is the exception rather than the rule. We don't have to look back very far to remember an era when this wasn't the case.

During World War II, the American government encouraged citizens to plant "victory gardens" as a way to alleviate pressure on the public food supply, and also as a means of boosting morale by creating

the feeling that ordinary people could make a contribution to the war effort. What is less discussed is the fact that more than 20 million people grew such gardens, and in 1944 alone, they managed to grow the equivalent of 40 percent of all the vegetable produce consumed in the country. This example demonstrates quite clearly the impact that regular folks can make when enough of us pitch in.

There is a long and diverse list of motivations that may be inspiring today's backyard farmers. The people who I talked

to during the process of writing this book cited, collectively, the following benefits:

- Obtaining better and fresher produce
- Saving fossil fuels related to food transportation costs
- Reducing the need for chemically based, potentially harmful fertilizers and pesticides
- Enjoying the pride and satisfaction of doing it yourself
- Building community by frequenting farmer's markets
- Supporting local businesses
- Building community by knowing the people who produce food and sharing with others
- Strengthening a secure network of food production: local farms are a key part of this

Some of these goals are easily attainable even on the individual level—anybody who has tasted a fresh, homegrown tomato harvested at its peak can attest to this. Other goals, such as trying to reduce fossil fuel consumption, need to be reached by a great many people in order for a positive impact to be perceived. It is worth remembering the huge effect produced by the victory gardeners half a century ago. I try to frame this kind of scenario in win-win terms: by growing as much of our own food as we can, we'll immediately enjoy the benefits of better food and stronger connections to our communities. I hope these fun and delicious incentives alone are powerful-enough motivators to get more people involved so that significant gains can be made on a global level.

Today's backyard farm may not fit the preconceived ideals that we attach to the word "farm," and for good reason. Few of us—especially those of us who live in urban environments—have enough space to accommodate long uniform rows of crops, and most of the work in backyard farms is done by hand rather than by large machines. The good news is that these constraints don't have to limit you all that much: the key to success for today's backyard farmers is having or gaining the ability to adapt and plan cleverly so you can make the most of the space you do have. For many of us, this means implementing container gardens and making efficient use of land through vertical gardening practices. It isn't hard to extend the growing season with cloches, greenhouses, and cold frames. To enjoy the fruits of your labors all year long, you may wish to look into canning and preserving your produce. This can be easier than you think—my friends make homemade fruit roll-ups every year from their apricots using a simple solar dryer that they made with free materials.

planning your garden

How much space will you need to have a meaningful backyard farm? The answer, of course, depends on how many people you're trying to feed and what you're trying to grow. For most of us, answering this question will take some trial and error. There are so many factors (soil and weather, just to name a couple) that can influence your results, and you'll likely see fluctuations from year to year. Some crops will exceed your expectations, and some might disappoint. In other words, it is inherently pretty tricky to pin down empirical data that guarantees the type of yield you'll get from a given sized garden plot, but I'm going to present some

 If you grow too much produce, share with the local food bank.

generalizations for a reasonable jumping-off point. See the chart at right for a list of popular veggies and how many plants you'll need per person.

square foot gardening

One really popular garden planning method that has received a ton of attention since it was first publicized in the early 1980s is the square foot gardening concept. In his book of the same name, author Mel Bartholomew advocates a simple but extremely efficient system for growing vegetables in 4' x 4' (1220 x 1220mm) raised beds. His approach eliminates wasted space between plants, which means that his plots produce the same amount of food as traditional row-planting, while requiring only 20% as much space. If you apply his principles, he suggests that you can expect the following results:

One 4' x 4' (1220 x 1220mm) box will supply enough produce to make a salad for one person every day of the growing season.

A second 4' x 4' (1220 x 1220mm) box will supply the daily supper vegetables for that person.

A third 4' x 4' (1220 x 1220mm) box will supply that person with extra produce to preserve or give away.

Mr. Bartholomew further specifies that a typical 4' x 4' (1220 x 1220mm) box should provide, in one spring season, the following very impressive list of crops:

- One head of cabbage
- One head of broccoli
- One head of cauliflower
- Four heads of romaine lettuce
- Four heads of red lettuce
- Four heads of leaf lettuce, followed by sixteen scallions
- Four heads of salad lettuce
- Five pounds (2¼kg) of sugar peas
- Eight bunches of Swiss chard
- Nine bunches of spinach, then nine turnips
- Sixteen small, ball carrots
- Sixteen beets, plus four bunches of beet greens
- Sixteen long carrots
- Thirty-two radishes

For more information on this great gardening technique, see Mel Bartholomew's book *All New Square Foot Gardening*.

As mentioned before, many factors will come into play when planting a garden, but I'm hoping the following chart will provide a good starting point. It gives measurements indicating how much space you should provide for one plant of each kind listed. These measurements are

guidelines to get you planting. As you gain more experience, you'll discover you can adjust some of the numbers to fit your gardening space and needs. Experimenting is a great way to figure out how you can get everything you want out of your garden.

I think that it is abundantly clear that growing at least some of your own food is a terrific undertaking, as seen from many different perspectives. And while we all have our own unique motivations and approaches, it is my goal in this book to highlight the pleasures of backyard farming, and to provide a lot of detail about the kinds of structures that you can easily build to make the entire process more efficient. The projects that I have presented here are designed to help your backyard farm grow more produce in less space and with less work. I have also included a number of in-depth profiles of some of my own backyard farming heroes in the hope that you'll find them as inspiring and interesting as I do.

Here's to a bumper crop!

Chris Gleason
Salt Lake City, Utah
June 2011

VEGETABLE PLANTS NEEDED PER PERSON

vegetable	amount per person	area needed per plant
Asparagus	5–10 plants	48 sq. in. (310 sq. cm.)
Beans	10–15 plants	10 sq. in. (64 sq. cm.)
Beets	10–25 plants	12 sq. in. (77 sq. cm.)
Bok Choy	1–3 plants	5 sq. in. (32 sq. cm.)
Broccoli	3–5 plants	36 sq. in. (232 sq. cm.)
Brussels Sprouts	2–5 plants	24 sq. in. (155 sq. cm.)
Cabbage	3–5 plants	12 sq. in. (77 sq. cm.)
Carrots	10–25 plants	10 sq. in. (64 sq. cm.)
Cauliflower	2–5 plants	18–24 sq. in. (116–155 sq. cm.)
Celery	2–8 plants	18 sq. in. (116 sq. cm.)
Corn	10–20 plants	12 sq. in. (77 sq. cm.)
Cucumber	1–2 plants	12 sq. in. (77 sq. cm.)
Eggplant	1–3 plants	18–24 sq. in. (116–155 sq. cm.)
Kale	2–7 plants	18–24 sq. in. (116–155 sq. cm.)
Kohlrabi	3–5 plants	2–5 sq. in. (13–32 sq. cm.)
Leafy Greens	2–7 plants	12 sq. in. (77 sq. cm.)
Leeks	5–15 plants	12–36 sq. in. (77–232 sq. cm.)
Lettuce, Head	2–5 plants	12–18 sq. in. (77–116 sq. cm.)
Lettuce, Leaf	10–15 plants	2–4 sq. in. (13–26 sq. cm.)
Melon	1–3 plants	48–72 sq. in. (310–465 sq. cm.)
Onion	10–25 plants	12–24 sq. in. (77–155 sq. cm.)
Peas	15–20 plants	18–24 sq. in. (116–155 sq. cm.)
Peppers, Bell	3–5 plants	18–24 sq. in. (116–155 sq. cm.)
Peppers, Chili	1–3 plants	18 sq. in. (116 sq. cm.)
Potatoes	5–10 plants	24–36 sq. in. (155–232 sq. cm.)
Radishes	10–25 plants	2–4 sq. in. (13–26 sq. cm.)
Squash, Summer	1–3 plants	24–36 sq. in. (155–232 sq. cm.)
Squash, Winter	1–2 plants	84–144 sq. in. (542–929 sq. cm.)
Tomatoes	1–4 plants	48 sq. in. (310 sq. cm.)
Zucchini	1–3 plants	36 sq. in. (39 sq. cm.)

 Each year, the UK hosts a National Giant Vegetable Championship.

WASATCH COMMUNITY GARDENS
Salt Lake City, Utah

Wasatch Community Gardens (WCG) is a non-profit group with a mission to empower people of all ages and incomes to grow and eat healthy, organic, local food. This mission supports and celebrates urban farming in a number of ways, and I spoke with Community Educator Carly Gillespie to learn more.

community gardens

As their name suggests, WCG operates seven community gardens where people can rent plots to grow their own vegetables. Because not everyone who wants to garden has a viable backyard of their own, this program has been immensely successful, and it is growing all the time. It currently involves over 180 families per year. WCG also functions as an umbrella organization for the Community Garden Network, which operates 20 community gardens in the area and assists new ones in forming. It offers quite a bit of assistance, including free vegetable and herb seedlings and seeds, 10 hours of Wasatch Community Gardens consulting time, and access to other discounted and free resources (compost, materials, tools, seeds, etc), as available. In 2011, Wasatch Community Gardens contributed more than

$15,000-worth of materials to community gardens in the Network. Membership in the Network also grants member gardens access to financial assistance, as available: in 2011, Wasatch Community Gardens will contribute $14,000 in mini-grants to new and developing community gardens in the network.

backyard sharing

In addition to their work with community gardens, WCG also utilizes another innovative program that helps gardeners find land. Working under the theory that there is enough viable land in the community, but much of it is not being

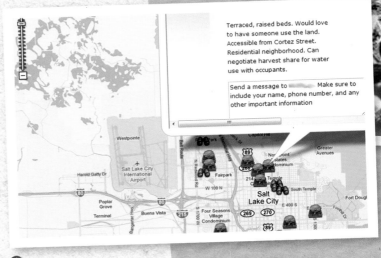

Terraced, raised beds. Would love to have someone use the land. Accessible from Cortez Street. Residential neighborhood. Can negotiate harvest share for water use with occupants.

Send a message to ▬▬▬ Make sure to include your name, phone number, and any other important information

⬆ Sharing backyards. There is plenty of land that is not being utilized to its full potential, and this Web site helps backyard farmers find plots for gardening. Visit www.sharingbackyards.com.

↑ Gardening as a community can bring joy, knowledge, and vegetables to a lot of people!

Try heirloom tomatoes sliced and lightly sprinkled with salt and pepper. You'll be amazed by the delicious flavor.

properly utilized, WCG encourages people to participate in backyard sharing. The initiative is remarkably simple but the implementation—a clever online tool by LifeCycles—makes it really effective. People who are willing to share their yards with local gardeners post their location and some other information, and this database is visible to people who are looking for a place to plant some seeds. It is an ingenious program that essentially runs itself—Carly jokingly referred to it as "Craigslist for Farmers"—but it is a fantastic way to support a potentially very powerful movement. Visit *www.sharingbackyards.com* to check it out.

community education

The other major component of WCG's mission relates to community education. Carly provided a lot of information about how much this has grown over the years. For many years, the group put on about a dozen workshops per year; then, in 2009, they aimed for 20 workshops to coordinate with their 20th anniversary. Just two years later, they hosted 35 workshops and served over 1,000 participants. There has obviously been a huge interest! Carly also stressed that all of the growth has been organic and based on the interest of the community, which makes sense. If your goal is to serve people's needs, offer the kind of things that they'd like to attend! Here is a partial list of the kinds of workshops they

present regularly: fall planting workshop; the legend of the three sisters (growing corn, beans, and squash together); fun with fungi; garlic planting and growing; fall seasonal cooking; beginning organic gardening; winter composting; eating locally for the holidays; garden planting and design; chicken week (includes coop tours, seminars, and more); beekeeping workshop; rainwater harvesting; building structures for your garden; cultivating fruit trees; the year-round garden; gardening in small spaces; seed selecting and starting.

Their educational programs also focus on the younger folks in the community. Wasatch Community Gardens serves 1,500 urban youth, ages 3–18, in its youth programs each year. City Roots Youth Gardening Classes, City Sprouts Summer Camps, field trips, and the Junior Farmers program take place at two of their teaching gardens,

⬆ Workshops and classes aplenty instruct local gardeners in everything there is to know about gardening.

↑ The Wasatch Community Gardens' annual plant sale disperses more than 30,000 plants in a single day.

the Fairpark Garden and the Grateful Tomato Garden. In 2011:

- 520 elementary school-aged students participated in after-school and summer classes
- 574 teens participated in community service in the garden
- 392 elementary school-aged students visited the garden on field trips
- 1851 pounds (840 kg) of produce were harvested from the youth gardens (food given to students, their families, and food pantries)
- 27 partner agencies brought youth participants to the gardens

plant sale

And finally, WCG also puts on an enormous plant sale every spring, a fun social event that serves as a kick-off to the growing season for thousands of people. The sale supports WCG's work and provides local growers with an astonishing variety of organic vegetable

seedlings, including over 50 varieties of heirloom tomatoes. They sell over 30,000 plants in a single day.

finding a community garden in your area

One of the easiest ways to locate community gardens is—perhaps not surprisingly—online. There are a number of Web sites dedicated to this pursuit, and here are links to some particularly good ones:

- **The American Community Gardening Association** (ACGA)
  www.communitygarden.org
- **Local Harvest** (also has links to farmer's markets and more)
  www.localharvest.org
- **Wikipedia**
  Do a search for "community gardening in the United States" or wherever you are
- **Federation of City Farms & Community Gardens** (in the UK)
  www.farmgarden.org.uk
- **City Farmer News** (based in Canada but has stories about urban farming everywhere)
  www.cityfarmer.info

The above resources have state-by-state listings of existing community gardens, and lots of other related info. You could also find one the old-fashioned way: ask around at local garden centers, green houses, natural food stores, or co-ops.

For instant gratification, have your kids plant some radishes; they'll come up in a matter of days.

HOW DOES YOUR GARDEN GROW?
Garden Upkeep

Before you can plant a garden, you have to have a spot ready for your plants. That means building a bed; I recommend a raised one—there are two examples in this chapter. That also means preparing an irrigation and rainwater collection system. Constructing a vermiculture bin to help worms flourish will also pay off in well-maintained soil around your crops' root systems. Get these foundational steps out of the way so your garden can produce at top level.

**building projects for the
BACKYARD FARMER**

RAINWATER HARVESTING SYSTEM
Collect and Save Rainwater for Your Garden

My family lives in a dry area—Salt Lake City, Utah, to be precise—and people in this region frequently worry about the threat of drought. Most of our municipal water comes from snow melt in the nearby mountains, and while we've been fortunate to have seen some pretty big snowfalls in recent years, a bad year could pose real problems for the million-plus people who call the area home. And it isn't just the west that has water worries: the southeast endured a serious drought a couple of years ago, and people all over the country are realizing that it makes sense to lessen our dependence on the municipal water supply. This trend appeals even more to today's urban farmers, who often have a do-it-yourself streak to begin with.

Note: Rainwater harvest systems like this are ideal for watering gardens, but they are not to be used for drinking water. This simple rain barrel doesn't offer any means to purify the water to the level required for direct human consumption.

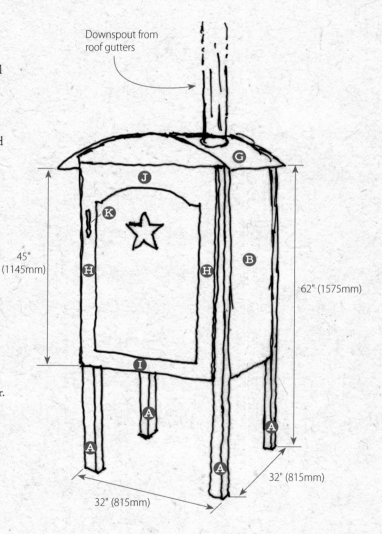

Downspout from roof gutters

45" (1145mm)

62" (1575mm)

32" (815mm)

32" (815mm)

Check in with your local water company. Many places offer incentives for rainwater collection, including free storage barrels.

RAIN BARREL MATERIALS LIST

	item	materials	dimensions	quantity
A	Legs	2x2 (38 x 38mm)	62" (1575mm)	4
B	Side panels	⅜" (8mm) plywood	45" x 32" (1145 x 815mm)	2
C	Back panel	⅜" (8mm) plywood	45" x 32" (1145 x 815mm)	1
D	Floor cleats	2x4 (38 x 89mm)	32" (815mm)	2
E	Floor panel	¾" (17mm) plywood	30" x 29" (760 x 740mm)	1
F	Top rail	¾" (17mm) plywood	32" x 6" (815 x 150mm)	2
G	Door panel	⅜" (8mm) plywood	45" x 32" (1145 x 815mm)	1
H	Door stiles	1x3 (19 x 63mm)	44" (1120mm)	2
I	Door bottom rail	1x3 (19 x 63mm)	25" (635mm)	1
J	Door top rail	1x6 (19 x 140mm)	25" (635mm)	1
K	Door handle			1
L	Door hinges			1 pair
M	Roof	⅛" (3mm) plywood	40" x 36" (1015 x 915mm)	1
N	Roof supports	¾" (17mm)-thick plywood	32" x 7" (1145 x 178mm)	2
O	55-gallon (208-liter) barrel with lid			1
P	Downspout fittings as needed			
Q	Hose bib			1
R	Neoprene washer			1
S	Threaded valve			1
T	Filter			1
	Screws			

a few words on water use

As I researched this chapter, I got interested in the way my family and I use water in and around our home, and I learned a lot. For one thing, we use a lot of water! Much less than the average for our area, but it still seemed like a lot to me. To determine how much water you use every year, I highly recommend checking out an online water-use calculator. It is eye-opening, to say the least. The basic calculations will only take a few minutes, and it will provide a frame of reference for discussing using water in your garden.

In the interest of full disclosure: my household estimated water use is around 40,000 gallons (151, 415 liters) per year, so the 55-gallon (208 liter) system that I built for this chapter won't make a dent in our overall water use. As I'll demonstrate, however, even collecting water from a small shed roof, as this system does, provides 25–30% of the water that we need annually for our garden. So, from that perspective, it is something to feel good about.

how much rainfall can you collect?

To determine the amount of water that you could potentially collect during the year, just follow these steps. (See Rainfall Calculation Worksheet on page 22.)

1. First figure out the square footage of the roof. You want the width times the length.
2. Convert the square footage into square inches by multiplying by 144.
3. Multiply the square inch measurement of your roof by the average annual inches of rainfall for your area. This number is how many cubic inches of rain will fall on your roof in a year.

4. Finally, convert the cubic inches into gallons by dividing the number by 231 (that's how many cubic inches are in a gallon).

EXAMPLE

So, using my shed roof as an example:

1. I'm using one half of my shed roof, which measures 15' x 7', or 105 square feet.
2. 105 square feet multiplied by 144 yields 15,120 square inches.
3. The annual rainfall in Salt Lake City is 16 inches per year. 16 inches of rain multiplied by 15,120 square inches of roof area yields 241,920 cubic inches of rain.
4. 241,920 cubic inches of rain divided by 231 cubic inches in a gallon yields 1,047 gallons of water a year.

EFFICIENCY

It is important to point out that no rainwater collection system is 100% efficient, as evaporation, run-off, and leaks will have some effect. Most estimates state that you can plan on capturing 70–90% of the amount of rain that falls. So, in this case, harvesting 80% of the rainfall would yield 837 gallons per year. That would seem to indicate a need for several 55-gallon (208-liter) barrels to ensure that I'm able to collect all of the available rainfall; but, in reality, less capacity is probably just fine, since the rainfall and usage are both spread across the whole year. As rain comes down, I'm really only storing it for a fairly short time before using it, so I don't need a year's worth of capacity.

With this in mind, I figured that I have a couple of options. A single (55 gallon) barrel system would probably be adequate, since I planned on using the water pretty frequently, and rainstorms are not particularly common in this area. To be safe,

---

Harvesting rainwater can reduce run-off and erosion, and prevent surface water contamination.

a double-barrel system would probably provide enough extra capacity to ensure that I was able to capture all of the rainfall without losing out due to an already-full barrel. As an experiment, however, I decided to start with one barrel and see how that worked out, figuring that I could always add more barrels later on. One year later, it seemed to work fine.

Not sure how much rain your area receives in a year? I wasn't either, but the information is just a quick Internet search away.

And, how much water will your garden need over the course of a season? Rules of thumb are tricky when it comes to guesstimating water usage because

variations in climate, soils, and the plants themselves will make a big difference. As a general guideline, however, you can figure that watering with sprinklers (or a hose), one time per week in the amount of 1–2 inches (25–50 mm) of moisture will require 65–130 gallons (246–492 liters) per 100 square feet (9.3 square meters). Note that drip irrigation will generally provide a more efficient use of water, as less is lost to evaporation, and the water is targeted directly to the plants that you're trying to cultivate.

RAINFALL CALCULATION WORKSHEET

_____ length of roof x _____ width of roof = _____ square footage of roof

_____ square footage of roof x 144 square inches in a foot = _____ square inches on roof

_____ square inches on roof x _____ inches of rainfall per year = _____ inches of rainfall on roof per year

_____ inches of rainfall on roof per year / 231 square inches in a gallon = _____ gallons of water fall on roof per year

_____ gallons of water fall on roof per year x .8 efficiency in collection = _____ gallons of water actually collected from roof per year

choosing a type of system

The type of rainwater harvesting system that you decide to build will depend, like most things, on what you're trying to accomplish and what you are willing to spend. To get the most that Mother Nature has to offer, you'll want to maximize both your collection and storage. If you live in a wet area, such as the Pacific Northwest, you may be able to harvest enough rain to meet your household's needs for 8–10 months out of the year for as little as just a couple of thousand dollars. To cite one example from the *Portland Online* Web site, a large-scale cistern with a capacity of 1,500 gallons (5,678 liters), drawing from a large roof top in a wet area, can easily store 25,000 gallons over the course of a year. That's a lot of water; about 60% of what my household uses in a year. Pretty impressive! At the other end of the spectrum, a single barrel system will help provide a good portion of the water that your garden will need, at a cost of $50–100. Where do you hope to land on this continuum? I recommend doing some more in-depth research to help you decide, but I hope this discussion can provide some food for thought to get you started.

GRAVITY SYSTEM

The simplest type of system utilizes gravity to do all the work. Gutters collect rainwater and channel it into a barrel, and a hose at the bottom of the barrel can be moved around to draw on the water supply as needed. If you position the barrel up on a stand in a location where the barrel is higher than the beds you plan to water, this is probably all the water pressure you'll need. Remember that the higher the water, the more water pressure will be generated. You cannot just stick a hose in a barrel, start a siphon, and expect it to keep flowing—unless the water source is higher than where you are directing the end of the hose.

DRIP IRRIGATION SYSTEM

Even though rain barrels are pretty simple, they do offer a choice in watering methods: you can simply water with a hose, or, by adding on inexpensive kits available online, you can use barrels for drip irrigation. Drip irrigation kits are important if you plan to use rain barrels without a pump, because most drip systems require much higher pressure than a gravity-fed system can generate. To compensate for this, several manufacturers have created kits that still allow you to enjoy the efficiency of drip irrigation without the need for an electric pump. Here are a couple of suppliers that I recommend checking out, but be sure to do some Internet searching to see if there is a local source for your needs:

www.irrigationdirect.com
www.flotender.com
www.rainbarrelman.com

If you decide to use a drip kit, just follow the manufacturer's directions and you should be up and running quickly and easily.

Rainwater is free of salt, which harms plant roots.

1 **Choose a spot.** The most logical layout should be pretty intuitive: since you'll be harvesting the rainwater that falls onto a roof, you'll want to identify the roof pitch that is in the best spot, and where a barrel might be placed. Unless you are interested in building a more complex system with an electric pump, the barrel will need to be situated above the area that you'll be watering—this factor alone may make your decision for you. For us, we had an out of control rose bush that looked nice, but wasn't providing anything edible, so we decided to clear it out and put in a rain barrel and raised bed. The hardest part was getting around to it. Once I got going, it only took about half an hour to prep the site. This is definitely a project that I should've done years ago.

2 **Measure the barrel.** I began the actual construction by measuring our barrel—a standard 55-gallon (208-liter) barrel (O) we obtained for free from a local brewery. This determined the size of the enclosure required.

3 **Attach the side panels to the legs.** The enclosure I built was super simple, but it is very sturdy and it has held up quite well. It consists of two identical plywood side panels (B) that are each screwed to a pair of 2x2 (38 x 38mm) legs (A).

4 **Attach the two side assemblies.** I connected the two side panel assemblies to each other by running a back panel (C) between them and fastening it into place with screws. I did the work with the whole assembly laid down on the floor because it was easier to work with gravity rather than fight against it.

5 Install floor cleats. The enclosure needed a very strong floor because a full barrel is heavy—over 400 pounds (181kg). To support the floor panel, I attached a set of 2x4 (38 x 89mm) cleats (D) to the sides (B) and to the legs (A) with screws. A clamp held them in place temporarily.

6 Install the floor. The floor panel (E) itself was made of ¾" (17mm) plywood. I screwed it securely into the cleats (D). If you're after a really Spartan look, you could probably just stop here. This ultra-simple assembly would probably work fine, although you might want to reinforce the top of the structure to keep the whole thing from wobbling. The roof actually helps to make the whole thing a lot more rigid.

7 Assemble the door. This door was built very simply from a ⅜" (8mm) plywood panel (G) and dressed up with a frame (H–J) made from 1x3s that I screwed directly to the front of the panel. Dress up the door however looks good to you. I cut the top rail in an arch shape for decorative purposes.

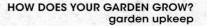

Watering your lawn or garden yourself instead of using sprinklers can cut your water consumption in half.

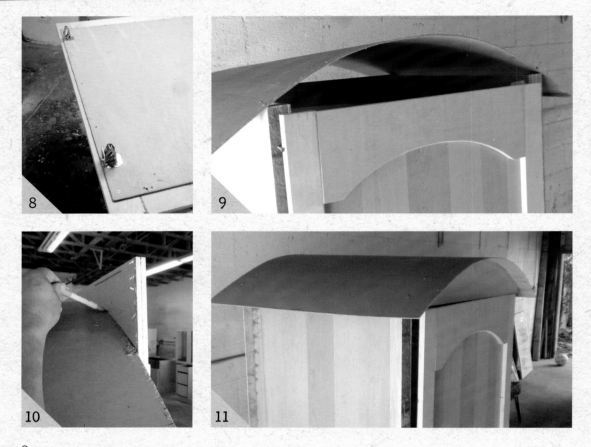

8 Attach the hinges. This door was attached with simple concealed hinges (L) because I had them laying around. Use whatever works for you.

9 Establish the roof curve. The unique curved roof of the enclosure is made from ⅛" (3mm) plywood (M) held in place on the ends by a pair of corresponding ¾" (17mm)-thick plywood supports (N). To determine the shape of the roof, I bent the panel into an eye-pleasing curve and tacked the corners with screws.

10 Mark the roof curve. To scribe the profile onto the supports (N), I simply held them up and traced the shape of the curve onto the back of the supports. I used a band saw to cut them to size.

11 Attach the roof. The completed supports (N) were then screwed to the stilts (A). With the supports in place, it was pretty easy to put the roof (M) back on and run screws through the roof panel and into the edge of the supports. The result was really sturdy, and it helped keep the whole thing light enough to move around with ease. The curved shape allowed me to create a very strong roof that shed snow very readily, even though the material itself was surprisingly thin. It has survived two very snowy winters in perfect condition.

12

13

14

15

12 Dress up the project. Since our enclosure is quite visible in our backyard, I decided to dress it up a bit. The use of paint will also help these materials last a lot better outdoors. Here's the barrel in its final location. Time to get it hooked up.

13 Hook up the system. Plumbing the barrel is really simple—you just need to add an extension (P) to the gutters so that water drains into the barrel (O). This will probably require a flexible connector, depending on where exactly your barrel is positioned.

14 Install the threaded valve. The water will drain from the barrel (O) via a simple threaded valve (S) that will attach to a standard garden hose. If your barrel has a hole in it at the bottom, size the valve to fit that. If not, use a twist drill bit on a power drill to create a hole. Make sure you put scrap wood behind where you're drilling to keep the drilling steady. Make sure to install the valve with a neoprene washer (R) to keep water from leaking around the hole.

15 Install a filter. A filter (T) is required somewhere along the line to keep large chunks of debris out of the water. I used a wire filter that goes right on top of the drain hole in the gutter.

Mawsynram, Meghalaya, India, gets the most rain, with 467" (11,873 mm) of rain per year.

IRRIGATION STRATEGIES
Find the Best System for Your Garden

Depending on where you live and what you're trying to grow, you might just get lucky and find a vegetable that doesn't require much in the way of water. It sure would be nice if we could just let nature take its course and effortlessly enjoy a nice harvest! However, most of us will need to put some time and energy into watering our crops if we're going to have results to be excited about. In our region—my family lives in Salt Lake City—we get almost no rain during the summer, so irrigation is a pretty hot topic around here.

overhead watering

The simplest form of irrigation is overhead watering, which usually means spraying plants with a hose. This works, but it has a couple of important downsides. For one thing, it wastes a lot of water due to evaporation, overspray, and an inability to really target the places where water is most needed. Additionally, it can encourage disease by allowing too much water to settle on and around the plants. More effective methods use much less water and are better for the overall health of your plants.

The two main types of irrigation that you'll likely want to consider for your own backyard farming efforts involve soaker hoses and drip lines. The systems are similar in that they'll both save you a ton of time and money, and you'll soon establish an easy routine for watering once you've gotten some experience and seen how the system works.

drip irrigation

Drip irrigation is a system of tubing with offshoots—you can put an emitter right alongside each plant you want to be watered. The emitters slowly drip water into the soil at the root zone. This is a good way to water vegetables that are spaced far apart as well as container gardens on a deck or terrace. Water is dispersed at low pressure wherever the tubes are placed. This irrigation method is typically more than 90% efficient at allowing plants to use the water applied, unlike other forms of irrigation, such as sprinklers, that are only 65–75% efficient. Kits for drip systems are available at garden centers and through garden suppliers. Drip systems contain a lot of different parts, so buying one is an investment that does have an upfront cost.

⬆ Drip tape is perfectly suited for row crops,
as illustrated here. It is inexpensive, it
can operate at very low pressure, and it
distributes water evenly, which means you
can plant some pretty long rows.

Drip irrigation systems put water directly at plants' roots, where they need it.

project

GARDEN CART
Large Capacity, No-Tip Wheelbarrow

Having a backyard farm means moving a lot of stuff around, especially in the spring, as beds are being prepared for the upcoming growing season. I used to use a wheelbarrow to assist in these chores, but I frankly got sick of it constantly tipping over. I also felt like it didn't have quite enough carrying capacity. These limitations got me thinking, and I came up with this design that I'm really happy with. Because it has two wheels, this garden cart is virtually impossible to tip over—a real blessing, as you'd know if you've ever accidentally spilled a load of horse manure in the wrong place! It holds a lot more material than most wheelbarrows, and is easy to load and unload because one side is left open. The large diameter wheels (they're 26" [660mm] wheels from a bike I bought at a thrift store) roll smoothly over obstacles and rough surfaces.

Note: I originally chose to attach the wheels using a pair of beefy lag bolts. While this method seemed to be holding up fine, it did seem like a potential weak link over time, so I replaced the bolts with a ⅜" (10mm)-diameter threaded rod. Instructions for both options are included here.

**building projects for the
BACKYARD FARMER**

 The waterproof glue used to create marine-grade plywood helps keep the wood from warping or buckling.

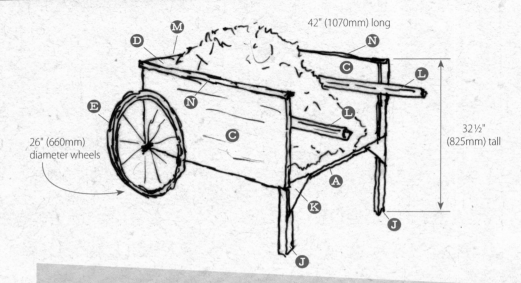

42" (1070mm) long

26" (660mm)
diameter wheels

32½"
(825mm) tall

GARDEN CART MATERIALS LIST

item	materials	dimensions	quantity
A Bottom panel	¾" (17mm) marine-grade plywood	42" x 30½" (1065 x 775mm)	1
B Reinforcing strips	2x2 (38 x 38mm)	42" (1065mm)	2
C Side panels	¾" (17mm) marine-grade plywood	42" x 20¼" (1065 x 515mm)	2
D End panel	¾" (17mm) marine-grade plywood	30½" x 18" (775 x 460mm)	1
E Bike wheels		26" (660mm) diameter	2
F Wheel axle option A	⁵⁄₁₆" (8mm)-diameter lag bolt	12" (305mm)	2
G Wheel axle option B	⅜" (10mm) diameter threaded rod	48" (1,220mm) cut down to fit	1
H Washer for wheel axle option B	⅜" (10mm) diameter		2
I Lock washer for wheel axle option B	⅜" (10mm) diameter		2
J Legs	2x2 (38 x 38mm)	32½" (825mm)	2
K Triangular braces	½" (11mm) plywood	6" x 6" (150 x 150mm)	2
L Handles	2x2 (38 x 38mm)	36" (915mm)	2
M Top front edge	L-shaped aluminum stock	32" (815mm)	1
N Top side edges	L-shaped aluminum stock	44" (1,120mm)	2
Screws	1¼" (32mm)		
Screws	2½" (65mm)		

1 Construct the bottom piece. I built the cart from ¾" (17mm) marine-grade plywood, which I bought at a local resale shop specializing in reclaimed building materials. It was a great score—$1 for a 4' x 8' (1220 x 2440mm) sheet! To attach the side panels (C) to the bottom panel (A), I fastened a pair of 2x2 (38 x 38mm) strips (B) to the underside of each long edge.

2 Attach the side panels. I used 1¼" (32mm) screws to hold the side panels (C) to the 2x2s (B).

3 Attach the end panel. To secure the end panel (D), I screwed into it through the sides (C) and bottom (A) using 2½" (65mm) screws.

A garden cart is more stable than a wheelbarrow and can be used to easily transport heavy loads.

4 **Install wheel axle.** The wheels (E) are shown here being attached with long
5⁄16" diameter lag bolts (F) that run into the 2x2 (B). If you'd rather use a 3⁄8" (10mm)-
diameter threaded rod (G), make a pair of holes in the 2x2 (B) where you want the
wheels and run the rod all the way through.

5 **Tighten the wheels down.** The lags (F) should be tightened as much as
possible while still allowing the wheels (E) to spin freely. If installing the rod (G)
instead, place a washer (H) between each wheel (E) and the body of the cart; then,
tighten everything up using a lock washer (I) on each side.

6

6 Determine the leg height. To determine the height of the legs (J) that will hold the cart level, I ran a straight edge across the tops of the wheels (E) and measured down to the bottom panel (A). This measurement was 13½" (345mm).

7 Attach the legs. The strongest legs would extend from the top of the cart to the bottom. To establish this length, I added 13½" (345mm) to the height of the side panels (C), minus 2¼" (57mm), which is the thickness of the 2x2 (B) and bottom panel (A). I screwed the legs (J) to the inside of the side panels (C).

7

Avoid splintering by placing a piece of masking tape along your intended cutting line on the underside of the wood before you cut it.

project: Garden Cart

8 **Add braces.** These 6" (150mm) triangular braces (K) stiffen up the back side of the cart while still allowing for a large open area on the end.

9 **Attach the handles.** The handles (L) are 2x2 blanks about 36" (915mm) long. They only extend about 12" (305mm) past the end of the cart, since that is enough to get a hold of. Having a large portion of the handle inside the cart means you can get a stronger connection: with screws placed approximately 2" (50mm) apart, a longer handle means more screws.

10 Shape the handles. To make the handles (L) easy to grip, I used a small router with a 45° chamfering bit to ease the edges. A roundover bit would also be a good choice.

11 Reinforce the top edge. Using plywood for this kind of project is a smart move, but I was concerned that the exposed plywood edge might begin to delaminate with exposure to rain and snow. To prevent this, I bought some L-shaped aluminum strips (M, N) and cut them to fit the top edge. Mitering the corners was quick, and it looked nice as well. I secured the strips with a number of 1¼" (32mm) screws.

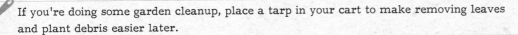

If you're doing some garden cleanup, place a tarp in your cart to make removing leaves and plant debris easier later.

COMPOST BOX
Sturdy Frame Opens On One Side

Seasoned gardeners develop their own approaches to composting, and their own box designs, but this simple box is a good way to get started. It has slatted sides and ends, so the air can circulate, and the front of the box lifts out, so you can turn the pile. When it's time to move the composted material into the garden, tip the box over and shovel the black gold. The box shown is big enough for a household's kitchen and garden waste, plus the autumn leaves from a couple of trees. You can refigure the box to any size you like, and if you make several of them, you'll have enough microbial spas to decompose the largest garden.

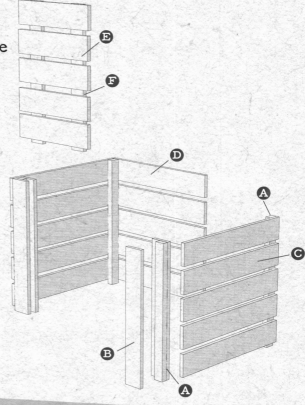

COMPOST BOX MATERIALS LIST

	item	materials	dimensions	quantity
A	Corner post	2x3 (38 x 63mm)	36" (915mm)	4
B	Flange	1x5 (19 x 114mm)	36" (915mm)	4
C	Side slat	1x6 (19 x 140mm)	36" (915mm)	10
D	Back slat	1x6 (19 x 140mm)	33" (840mm)	5
E	Front slat	1x6 (19 x 140mm)	24" (610mm)	5
F	Rail	1x4 (19 x 89mm)	36" (915mm)	2
	2½" (65mm) spiral nails or screws			

© John Kelsey. Designer: Ian Kirby. Photos, text, drawings: John Kelsey.

1 Make the corner posts and flanges. Saw the four corner posts (A) to their final length. Make the four flanges (B) the same length as the corner posts (A).

2 Nail the front posts. Align each flange piece (B) with the ends and one edge of the corner post (A), then attach it with five or six 2½" (65mm) spiral nails. Attach two flange pieces (B) to each front corner post (A). This makes U-shaped channels.

3 Nail the side slats to the front posts. Starting at the top of one front post (A), nail each side slat (C) to the post. Drive four of the 2½" (65mm) spiral nails into each intersection. Use a length of regular 1x2 (19 x 38mm) lumber to space the slats. Organize the side slats (C) so when you get to the bottom of the post, there's a 2–4" (50–100mm) space. Nail the second set of side slats (C) to the other front post (A) in the same way, but take care to make a right side and a left side.

4 Nail the side slats to the rear posts. Nail the free ends of the side slats (C) to each rear post (A). You should end up with two similar side panels, one right-handed and the other left-handed.

5 Nail the back slats to the sides. Stand the two completed side panels up on end, with the flanged front posts on the ground. Space the back slats (D) across the sides. Connect the two sides by squaring and fastening the top back slat in place. Nail the bottom back slat, then fill in the space with the remaining slats (D).

6 Make the front panel. Clench-nail (hammer over the end of the nail so it doesn't stick out) the front slats (E) to two rails (F). Make sure the front slats (E) will fit into the U-channeled front posts with ½" (13mm) clearance. Set the rails (F) in about 2" (50mm) from the ends of the slats so they don't interfere. Align the top slat with the end of the first rail (F) and drive the first nail. Then check for square and drive the remaining three nails. Attach the top slat to the other rail in the same way, measuring to be sure the rails remain parallel to one another. Fasten the bottom slat, then fill in with the remaining front slats (E). Clench all the nails on the back of the panel to ensure that the construction stays together until the wood itself rots.

Composting reduces yard waste volume by 50 to 75 percent.

RAISED BEDS 101
Here's Why You Want Them

Raised beds are an easy way to add more efficiency and beauty to your garden areas with just some old lumber and elbow grease. There are a number of reasons to incorporate them into your yard if you haven't already. Here are some of my favorites:

Create a pleasing design in your yard by installing raised beds that function as architectural elements, delineating zones within an overall landscape plan. They can serve as focal points, direct traffic flow, or define outdoor "rooms" for eating, relaxing, or entertaining.

Easily condition the soil through the addition of compost and other mix-ins so that you are not limited to what may be poor quality soil in a given location.

Set boundaries for plants that might otherwise take over. Our friends have a chocolate mint bush that has taken over vast swaths of their garden, so when we took some cuttings for our yard, we made sure to plant them in a raised bed where they won't get out of control.

Provide structure to attach trellises, hoop houses, and row covers, allowing you to obtain a larger yield and extend the growing season.

Work with comfort in beds that have been built to whatever height works for you. This is particularly useful for people who have limited mobility.

Achieve a higher density of plants. Because you don't have to allow areas to walk between rows of crops, you can plant vegetables closer together than in traditional ground beds. This means a larger harvest from a given area of land.

You don't need much space to install a raised bed-try putting some in that strip of grass between the sidewalk and the street.

Eliminate soil compaction, which can reduce crop yields up to 50 percent. Water, air, and roots all have difficulty moving through soil compressed by tractors, tillers, or human feet, and gardeners can avoid the problem completely by creating elevated beds narrow enough to work from the sides.

Drain off excess moisture better than ordinary garden beds. This is another advantage that helps the plant roots to breathe. In areas that have saturated soil, like Florida and many areas of the South, raised beds may be the only way you can grow many types of plants.

Create pest barriers against slugs and snails. Weeds are also less likely to pop up in a soil that you've blended yourself from compost, manure, and other ingredients.

⬆ Nail some planks to corner stakes for a quick raised bed.

⬆ The stacked corner raised bed is easy to make and quite sturdy (see page 52).

If gardening gives you knee or back pain, raise your beds a little higher to avoid bending down or kneeling.

EASY PLANK RAISED BEDS
Build Garden Plots from Reclaimed Lumber

There are a lot of ways to build raised beds. My favorite is to find a way to work with what I've got. In this case, I had a pile of Douglas fir boards that I salvaged when a neighbor removed a fence, and they were still in perfectly good shape. The major challenge of this project was working on the slope where we wanted to situate the beds: this made the process a little trickier, but it came out great in the end. This type of bed is a great way to start making raised bed—just grab some planks and something to serve as a corner post.

EASY PLANK RAISED BED MATERIALS LIST

	item	materials	dimensions	quantity
A	Corner posts	4x4 (89 x 89mm)		8
B	Long side boards	1x5 (19 x 114mm)	72" (1830mm)	12
C	Short side boards	1x5 (19 x 114mm)	60" (1525mm)	12
	Outdoor screws			
	Spar varnish			

You control the type of soil you use in your raised beds; a major bonus if you live in an area with poor gardening soil.

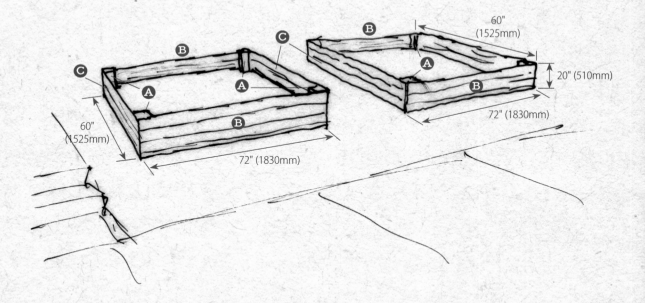

1 Prep the reclaimed lumber.
The most time-consuming part of the project was removing the nails from the lumber (B, C). This step was necessary, however, because we were going to run the boards through a planer and ruining the blades is a real concern if any fasteners remain.

2 Evaluate the lumber. Once the lumber (B, C) was de-nailed, we leaned it up along the wall so we could assess the quantity and lengths that we had to work with. Some of the boards had some paint left on them—we considered leaving it on, but ultimately we decided we were interested in natural wood finish all around.

3 **Gather the corner posts.** For corner posts, we cut up some 4x4s (A) that came from some shipping crates. I made sure to leave them extra-long at this point, as they would be trimmed to their exact heights after assembly.

4 **Plane the boards.** Planing the boards (B, C) is straightforward—it only took about five minutes to run the entire stack. You can skip this step if you don't have access to a planer, but it really does make assembling the pieces easier. It also makes the boards look a lot nicer—see the inset photo.

5 **Cut the sides to length.** We used a chopsaw to crosscut the boards (B, C) to length: we were making rectangular-shaped beds, so we needed an equal number of long sides and short sides.

Raised beds slow the spread of weeds and diseases through your garden.

project: Easy Plank Raised Beds

6 Take the pieces to the site. On site, we laid out a few of the boards (B, C) to get a sense of where to situate the beds and how it would look.

7 Assemble the front side. The easiest way to assemble the beds is to work in sections. I started by screwing the cross-pieces (C) to the corner posts (A), starting at the bottom. The rest of the front side went together quickly. I recommend using screws that are coated for outdoor use to prevent corrosion.

8 Attach the bottom boards. We were working on a slope, which was a little tricky. To make sure that things came together okay, I put the bottom boards on the whole bed, following the angle of the slope. There's no need for math here—just push the bottom boards down tightly against the ground to make sure that no soil will be able to leak out.

9 Check the corner posts. It is important to keep an eye on the corner posts (A) as you proceed—make sure that they stay plumb. I recommend sighting across them from time to time to make sure that they are parallel, because they can tend to shift around a little bit before they're fully secured.

6

7

8

9

10 Complete the beds. We built the second bed in the same manner as the first, making sure to leave enough space in the middle to walk around. This photo also illustrates why working on a slope makes it important to start out with posts that are extra-long. You can see here that the posts ended up at different heights, and there's no way to predict these dimensions beforehand. It is a lot easier to just give yourself more height than you'll need and cut off the excess later.

11 Trim the corner posts. I used a chainsaw to cut off the tops of the posts (A), but a reciprocating saw or even a handsaw would work, too.

12 Square the beds. It isn't critical that the final assemblies be square, but it is good practice to check. The best way to square a large object like this is to measure the diagonals and shift the bed around until the measurements are equal.

13 Varnish the boards. A coat or two of spar varnish is a good idea for two reasons: it will help the wood to last longer, and it also brings out a lot of the wood's natural beauty. For maximum durability, you might want to re-coat the beds every couple of years. It only takes a few minutes.

If space is tight, set up a small raised bed on your patio for herbs or small vegetable plants.

STACKED LUMBER RAISED BED
An Attractive and Sturdy Raised Bed Variation

I lucked into a supply of reclaimed redwood 2x4s (38 x 89mm) early in the season, and I decided to use some of them to build a new raised planting bed. Redwood is a great choice for this because it is naturally rot-resistant. Because I had such nice material to work with, and because I could be assured that the bed was likely to last for quite a long time, I decided to use a joinery method for the corners that would be very durable and attractive. I like the look of the staggered joints, and this approach can be used whether you're using 2x4 (38 x 89mm) or 4x4 (89 x 89mm) materials.

My friend Kate made this raised bed by setting the 2x4s on edge. This method is great because taller beds can be built with less lumber, and also less cutting. If you use this approach, you'll want to reinforce the corners with a post, as shown here.

 The drainage in raised beds is much better than in a standard garden.

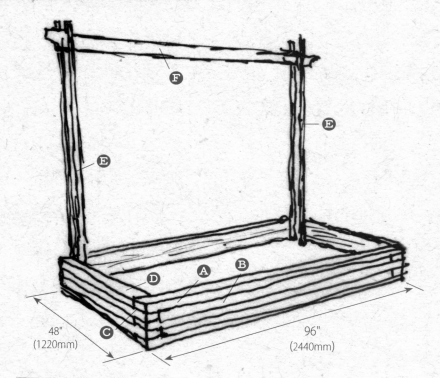

48"
(1220mm)

96"
(2440mm)

STACKED RAISED BED MATERIALS LIST

	item	materials	dimensions	quantity
A	Long sides	2x4 (38 x 89mm) or 4x4 (89 x 89mm)	96" (2440mm)	4
B	Short sides	2x4 (38 x 89mm) or 4x4 (89 x 89mm)	89" (2260mm)	3
C	Long ends	2x4 (38 x 89mm) or 4x4 (89 x 89mm)	48" (1220mm)	3
D	Short ends	2x4 (38 x 89mm) or 4x4 (89 x 89mm)	41" (1040mm)	4
E	Optional trellis, legs	2x2 (38 x 38mm)	Height as desired	4
F	Optional trellis, spanner	2x4 (38 x 89mm)	96" (2440mm)	1
	3" (75mm) deck screws			

1 **Figure out the size of the bed.**
I determined the size and location of the bed by setting out the first layer of 2x4s. When in doubt, start with lengths that are over-sized and cut them down until they fit the space the way you like. I listed measurements in the Materials List for a good-sized bed, but feel free to adapt these steps to whatever size bed you want.

2 **Cut the boards to length.** The work proceeds very quickly, and it only requires a couple of tools. The cuts can be made with a circular saw, or a chopsaw if you have one. My method for determining the required sizes is as follows (note that this bed measures 96" x 48" [2440 x 1220mm]).

There are four different lengths required, and here are the terms I employ to keep them separate. Each box requires long sides (A), short sides (B), long ends (C), and short ends (D). The long sides (A) are the same as the overall length of the bed—96" (2440mm) in this case. The long ends (C) are the same length as the overall width—48" (1220mm) in this case. The shorter components measure 7" (180mm) less than the overall lengths (each 2x4 is 3½" [90mm] wide). So, in this example, the short sides (B) are 89" (2260mm), and the short ends (D) are 41" (1040mm). This simple formula will work whether you're using 2x4s or 4x4s, although if you're using 2x4s set on edge, you'll subtract 3" (75mm) instead of 7" (180mm).

In addition to wood, you can construct a raised bed using concrete blocks, stone, or bricks.

3 Attach the layers. I used 3"
(75mm) deck screws to secure each
layer to the one below it, and I suggest
spacing the screws about 12" (305mm)
apart. To make sure that the fasteners
will hold up outside, you'll want to
use exterior-rated screws. This means
that they have a special weather-
resistant coating. Stainless steel screws
are also an option, but they're much
more expensive.

3

ADD A TRELLIS

1 Attach the posts. I decided to mount a trellis to the back of this bed so I could grow things vertically. I used 2x2 (38 x 38mm) lumber for the vertical components (E). I screwed it directly to the 2x4s (38 x 89mm) on the inside corners of the bed.

2 Attach the spanner. The vertical components (E) are spanned at the top by a 2x4 (F). Since I didn't have an assistant on this, I drove a screw near the top of the 2x2s (E) that I could set the 2x4 (F) on while I checked its position with a level. If one end was too high or low, it was easy to move the screw accordingly. Once the 2x4 (F) had been leveled, I screwed it to the 2x2s (E).

3 Add more support. To add more visual bulk to the trellis, I added a second 2x2 (E) in front of the 2x4 (F). This isn't functionally necessary—I just liked the look. I screwed the second 2x2 (E) into the side of the raised bed.

Try sprinkling chili powder along the edges of your raised beds to keep critters out.

KYLE LAMALFA

An Urban Farmer with a Broad Vision
Salt Lake City, Utah

Kyle LaMalfa is a major force in Salt Lake City's urban agriculture boom. Not only is he a farmer himself, growing a large amount of produce that he sells to a dedicated local client base, but he started the People's Market, which is a very popular venue for local food producers and artists.

catalyst for change

In 2004, Kyle took a class at the Westside Leadership Institute, a locally focused organization that helps people to develop skills they can use to improve their communities. The class project was to hold a community yard sale, and the success of this project was a real eye-opener for Kyle. He says that it was quite a big catalyst for change, and he began an exciting new chapter in his life. He began to think about an ongoing farmer's market for the city's west side.

the people's market

Kyle's planning paid off when the People's Market first opened in 2006. The goal was to have the market open for ten Sundays that summer. The venture was met with such enthusiasm that the vendors wanted to extend the season even longer.

The Market has grown significantly in the past five years—there are now almost 60

⬆ Kyle gets a jump on spring production using this hoop house he made from inexpensive flexible tubing. When it is covered with a layer of translucent plastic, the hoop house provides a nice warm place to get things growing much earlier than would be otherwise possible.

➡ Kyle is responsible for making homegrown produce available to many citizens of Salt Lake City.

The USDA reports 6,132 farmers' markets were in operation in 2010.

regular vendors, which is quite a jump from the initial 10 or 12, and the market has received a great deal of support from the community and local government. The Mayor's Office of Economic Development donated $16,000—this windfall was used, among other things, to invest in a machine that accepts food stamps. The People's Market was the first market in the area to do this, and the initiative clearly reflects Kyle's drive to make quality, locally produced food available to everyone. In addition to the weekend markets, the organization has three other popular annual events: a seed swap in January, a seedling sale and swap in May, and a crop swap in September.

the future

He's not stopping there: Kyle has all sorts of dreams for the future. He has a vision for a kitchen incubator—a licensed commercial kitchen that can be rented by groups and individuals who don't have the capital to invest in a kitchen of their own quite yet. Community groups and individuals would be able to use the facility on a pay-as-you-go basis. This would be a tremendous asset for food business start-ups, as there is currently no such place in the area. With ideas like this in his mind, and the wherewithal to see them through, it is no wonder Kyle is such an inspiration to those around him.

⬆ Keeping bees has become popular in the area during the past few years, and Kyle is proud of his setup. These two hives not only provide delicious honey, but they're a great way to ensure that his plants get pollinated.

⬆ Kyle showed me one of the simplest and most innovative trellising systems I've ever seen. He calls it the Florida weave. He begins by driving in a row of T-posts spaced about 5' (1525mm) apart, and then ties some nylon cord at the base. He runs the string between the posts, stopping to loop it around each post as he goes so that it won't sag later on. He creates five horizontal rows of string that provide sturdy support for the tomato plants that he'll grow in the garden bed below.

⬆ Always on the lookout for opportunities to grow more food, Kyle has turned this neglected strip of land into a fine row of beds for squash and other edibles. To maximize his efficient use of water, and to minimize the required labor, Kyle has set up a useful irrigation system.

Lancaster Central Market in Lancaster, Pennsylvania, is the oldest continuously operating farmers' market in the U.S.

POTATO PLANTER
Super-Efficient Way to Plant and Harvest Spuds

I had never tried growing potatoes, but when I heard about the potato box concept, I knew I had to give it a try. Some of the sources I found claim more than 100 pounds (45 kg) of potatoes can be grown in a compact 2' x 2' (610 x 610mm) area, so this method provides one of the most efficient gardening setups that I know about. The rule of thumb is 1 pound (.5 kg) of seed potatoes can yield 100 pounds (45 kg) of potatoes at harvest time. If you're trying to produce even more than that, this concept will scale quite easily: a 4', 6', or even 8' (1220, 1830, or 2440mm) potato bin could be built to multiply the bounty.

The technique is essentially a way to grow potatoes vertically, but not through the use of trellises, as is the case with many other plants. Instead, you simply build a box around a cluster of potato plants and, as they grow, cover them with mulch and straw. This forces the plants to grow ever higher, and they'll continue to set potatoes in the "underground" portion below the exposed foliage. You'll want to make sure to keep some of the leaves exposed—they do need to conduct photosynthesis, after all.

This potato box features modular sides that are screwed on as the plants grow taller, thus providing more space for your potato crop to develop. The slats don't have to be snug to each other, as the box itself can be filled in with straw and mulch—the main roots of the plants are established deeply in the ground, so the material you're using to fill in the bin as the plants grow functions more as a cover for the plants than as a nutritional medium. You'll want to prepare the ground below the planter, however, as that is the soil where the plants will establish themselves and draw nutrients from. Later in the season, you can remove the sides lower down on the box and steal some potatoes while the plants continue to grow, or you can just remove the screws and easily dig through the filler. This method has the advantage of not requiring a pitchfork be thrust into the ground, which often results in damaged potatoes.

While you can use ordinary potatoes from the grocery store that have begun to sprout, it is recommended that you

POTATO RATIO
1 pound (.5 kg) of seed potatoes can yield 100 pounds (45 kg) of potatoes at harvest time

The "Irish" white potato is actually native to South America's Andean Mountains.

plant seed potatoes that are known to be disease-free. Any good garden store should have them, and I paid less than $1.50 for a whole bunch. And since I used a couple of free shipping pallets to build the box, this project was among the most economical that I've ever built, too.

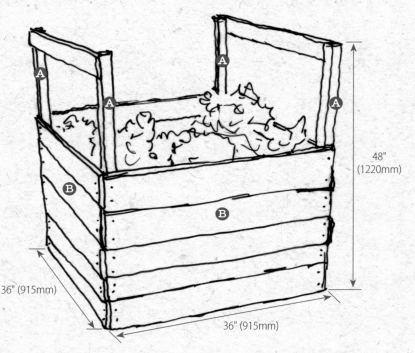

POTATO PLANTER MATERIALS LIST

All the materials I used came from 2 standard-size shipping pallets, but you could use standard lumber.

item	materials	dimensions	quantity
Ⓐ Posts	2x2 (38 x 38mm)	48" (1220mm)	4
Ⓑ Side strips	3½" to 4½" (90 to 115mm)-wide boards, ⅝" (16mm) thick	36" (915mm)	32
Screws			

1 **Gather your materials.** The humble pallet has many things to offer to a resourceful farmer. Its main advantage is probably its price: I don't mind having to do a little work to strip away the useful lumber when it costs nothing. If you'd rather use standard lumber or other scraps you have on hand, go right ahead—this project isn't too picky. I will continue to give tips for those of you utilizing pallets, though.

2 **Prepare the wood.** Pulling out every single nail, in my experience, is not usually worth the time and effort. It takes a long time, and it offers very little extra material, so I generally focus on the center sections, which have a lot fewer nails. A reciprocating saw, jigsaw, or circular saw can be used to quickly remove the nail-infested end portions of the pallet. This method leaves a number of fairly long (almost 36" [915mm]) strips of lumber from the center of the pallet.

Marie Antoinette once wore a crown of potato blossoms, drastically increasing the vegetable's popularity in Europe.

3 Free the boards. To separate the strips from the center support, I don't try to pull the nails—I've found that it is faster to remove the strips by twisting them. An angle grinder quickly cuts away any nails that remain, and a reciprocating saw does a great job of powering through any stubborn fasteners.

4 Rejoice in your pile of free lumber. This is the stack of lumber that I scavenged from two pallets. The boards are of varying widths, but they were uniform in length, and were free from splits, cracks, or other defects that would have limited their future uses.

3

4

5 Attach the first slat. The potato box is very easy to build—I took four pieces of 2x2 lumber that I scavenged from the pallet's thicker support pieces and used them as vertical corner posts (A). Screwing the first strips (B) to the posts was easiest when I set the posts down flat on the bench. It was much easier to ensure proper alignment between the parts. Assemble the planter someplace flat so that the assembly goes together straight and square. This will become important later on when you try to add the extra side pieces—if the frame is out of square, the boards won't fit!

6 Build two sides. I built two sides like this one. I used two strips (B) at the bottom to keep the assembly rigid, and one at the top to keep the posts (A) from splaying out irregularly. I also used a tape measure to verify that the diagonal measurements were equal—this indicated that the side panel was square.

7 Assemble the frame. I then attached a couple of strips to one of the side panels, and I finished by screwing the other side into place. The completed potato box is lightweight and easy to move around, so it doesn't have to be built on site if that isn't convenient.

Five potato plants were grown in space in 1995.

8 **Set up the planter.** Take the planter frame to where you want to grow your potatoes. Make sure that the placement of the bin allows access to all sides—I was tempted to push ours up against the fence, as an automatic reflex geared toward saving space in the yard, but you'll need enough room to screw the extra side pieces on as the potatoes grow, so bear this in mind when you situate yours. Dig up the soil a bit so you can sit the frame relatively flat on the ground. Plant the seed potatoes. My daughter, Abigail, at age three is already an avid gardener, and she couldn't resist hopping inside and doing some digging.

9 **Add slats as needed.** A few weeks in, the plants were well established and growing like crazy. After six weeks, I had added a number of tiers to the box so it was almost waist height. When the plants grow above the current highest slat, screw on the next level and fill up to that point with straw or mulch. Be sure to keep some leaves showing!

8

9

POTATO VARIETIES

There are countless varieties of potatoes, and each variety should be planted at a specific time of year. Here's some information about varieties you might want to include in your garden:

name	planting time	days to maturity	notes
AC Peregrine Red	Late season	100–120 days	Lasts a long time in storage
Caribe	Mid-season	55–70 days	Excellent baked
Goldrush	Late season	100–120 days	Good baked, mashed, in stews, or for perogies
Norland	Early season	70–85 days	Bright red skin
Red Pontiac	Late season	100–120 days	Drought-tolerant variety
Viking	Mid-season	85–100 days	Popular gardening variety
Yukon Gold	Mid-season	85–100 days	Great for perogies

According to the Guinness Book of World Records, the world's heaviest potato weighed in at 10 lb. 14 oz. (5kg).

TIERED LETTUCE RACK
This Handy Shelving Unit Will Increase Your Lettuce Yield

Fresh lettuce is one of my favorite things we grow in our backyard. It grows quickly, and when you're ready for a salad, just use kitchen shears to chop off the leaves that appeal to you. New leaves will usually grow back in their place, and we're generally able to get about three cuttings in this manner. After a while, I began to wonder if I could come up with a space-efficient way to grow them. Hence, the tiered rack was born. It is an inexpensive way to do some vertical gardening and get a nice yield from a small footprint.

The system is based around a series of shelves that are set back at the top of the rack and set forward at the bottom. This design helps as much sun as possible reach all the plants, as compared to a bookcase-style arrangement, which would cast a lot of shade. The sides of the rack are open, as well, for even more light exposure. I used ten containers from the dollar store (they measure approximately 15" x 5" x 5" [380 x 130 x130mm]), and the wood was free, so the total cost was quite economical. A few packets of seeds kept us in salads all summer long.

It is important to point out that the containers don't need to be very deep—most lettuces can be grown just fine in shallow containers—but you may need to water a bit more often, as moisture evaporates more quickly from containers than in-ground beds. I water quickly once per day, and it takes less than a minute.

LETTUCE VARIETIES

An important thing to remember when growing lettuce is that most varieties will wilt in hot temperatures, with the exception of Romaine. Here are some varieties you might want to try in your lettuce containers:

name	growing conditions	days to maturity	notes
Buttercrunch	Best in cool weather	75 days	Soft, loosely formed head
Salad Bowl	Best in cool weather	45 days	Sweet flavor
Romaine	Can grow in warm weather	45 days	Long cylindrical leaves
Boston	Best in cool weather	75 days	Head resembles a rose
Ruby	Best in cool weather	50 days	Dark red color
Bibb	Best in cool weather	75 days	From the same cultivar group as Buttercrunch

Season ground beef with Asian flavors like soy and hoisin sauce, garlic, ginger, shallots, and bean sprouts. Wrap the mixture in lettuce leaves for a new family meal.

1 Prepare the legs. I began the rack by ripping some long strips for the sides. I had a leftover maple board that I used to get four ¾" x 2" (20 x 50mm) strips (A). You could use a 1x2 or any other thin wood stock, though.

2 Position the legs. The sides are not symmetrical—in other words, the front leg slants back at an angle, while the rear leg is vertical—and I used a simple method for laying them out. By setting the parts on my workbench, I adjusted their positions until they looked about right. I didn't try to measure the angle of their intersection or anything complicated like that. Once I had the parts lined up, I placed the rear leg on top of the front leg: this made it easy to see where I would be removing material from the front leg.

3 Cut the leg angle. Mark the portion to be cut away. After making the cut with a jigsaw, the front and back legs fit together neatly. I also decided to remove a couple of inches of material from the top of the rear leg.

4 Adjust the front leg's foot. Before I attached the front and rear legs (A) to each other, I made sure to trim the bottom edge of the front leg so it would sit flat on the ground. This was done by simply making a visual observation—the portion that overhung the edge of the workbench was the portion that needed to be cut off.

5 Attach the legs. I used glue and nails to fasten the tops of the legs together. Any glue will work, but waterproof glue is the best—your shelf is going to be watered frequently unless it is under an overhang.

The average American consumes 30 lb. (14kg) of lettuce annually.

6 Make a second pair of legs.
I made a second side subassembly in the same way that I made the first one. You can start by laying the pieces for the second side (A) on top of the completed first side—that way they will match exactly.

7 Lay out the shelf locations. To lay out the locations of the shelves (G–K), I used a level and drew some lines across the front and rear legs (A). The exact distance between the lines (from one shelf to the next) isn't critical, as long as your containers (N) will fit. To transfer the marks to the second set of legs, I placed the sides on top of each other and extended the marks by eye.

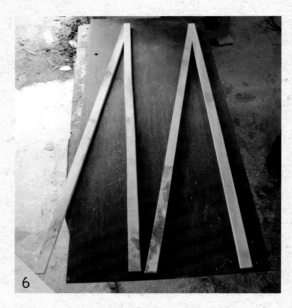

8 Create shelf supports. To support the sides of the shelves (G–K), I cut pairs of strips (B–F) to the lengths required and then nailed them to the sides. You could also use 1x2s for this. Because the shelves vary in terms of depth, I just measured directly across the sides to determine the lengths. The bottom shelf (K) was around 16" (405mm) deep, and the top one (G) was about 6" (150mm). Your shelves may be slightly different—just adjust the pieces to fit.

9 Attach backer panels. The whole thing began to take shape when I screwed a pair of ¼" (6mm) plywood panels (L) to the back of the rack. These panels provide a lot of rigidity to the finished unit. I could've cut out a back panel that was the size of the entire rack, but I didn't really see a need to: the rack was quite strong with just the two smaller ones.

10 Attach the shelves. The shelves (G–K) themselves were made of ⅜" (8mm) plywood. I screwed them directly into the supports (B–F) on the sides.

The Greeks served lettuce after a meal, believing it induced sleep. This tradition is continued today in Europe, where you receive your salad after your meal.

11 **Attach shelf front supports.** To keep the shelves (G–K) from sagging, I reinforced the front edges with hardwood strips (M).

12 **Prepare the planting containers.** To provide adequate drainage, I drilled some holes in the bottoms of the containers (N). Proceed slowly on this step so you don't crack that plastic. Putting a thick piece of scrap wood under the plastic to support the drilling isn't a bad idea either.

11

12

13 Add seeds. Here are the freshly seeded containers (N). You'll have a fresh, homegrown salad in as little as 30 days, depending on what varieties you select.

13

PLANTS THAT CAN BE GROWN VERTICALLY

Beans
Cantaloupes
Cucumbers
Grapes
Honeydew
Hops
Tomatoes
Peas
Potatoes
Pumpkins*
Squash
Watermelons*
Zucchini

*If you grow a plant with a large fruit, such as pumpkins or watermelons, you will have to add supports or shelves for the fruit as they develop.

There are four basic lettuce categories: Butterhead, Crisphead (Iceberg), Looseleaf, and Romaine (Cos).

WALL OF TOMATOES
Create a Living Wall of Tomatoes

I spent a few years growing tomatoes in cages with good results, but when I saw how building simple trellises could help tomatoes grow super tall, I was intrigued. While I hadn't really thought about it before, it turns out that tomatoes love to reach for the sky, and this has some great benefits in terms of keeping the plants healthy and ensuring a better-than-normal harvest.

One of my favorite benefits is that tomato walls look so great. My vision was to define different spaces in our yard by constructing hedges of tomato plants, and it really worked out well. This will be the method of tomato cultivation that I'll use from now on.

In addition to the main design, I've included photos of two additional tomato trellises we built in our yard this year. All three designs are pretty similar: two of them were anchored to raised beds, and one of them is freestanding, so you can decide for yourself which style suits your location the best. Also, I used a couple of systems to help support the tomatoes. On two of the trellises, I stretched thin plastic poultry netting, which is really inexpensive and easy to work with, and on the third trellis, I nailed horizontal strips to the support posts at 10" (255mm) increments. Both methods worked great.

For the netting, I just made sure to pull the stems through the holes in the wire mesh every so often; for the other trellis, I wove the stems back and forth between the strips as the plants grew. Both methods were really easy, although neither one offers quite the same "set it and forget it" approach that tomato cages do. That said, I actually like puttering around in the garden, so spending a few minutes per week weaving tomato stems into their support structure was a lot of fun. When it's time to clear the garden at the end of the growing season, the wooden rail support system really shows its worth—it is easy to remove the tomato plants. Poultry netting requires a lot more work with scissors to clear the plant matter, and it is difficult to reuse poultry netting from year to year—it tends to get damaged in the process of removing the vines. One caveat—make sure you select tomato varieties that are indeterminate (see sidebar 85). If you pick determinate types, they will not grow into a wall.

The tomato is the official state fruit and vegetable of Arkansas.

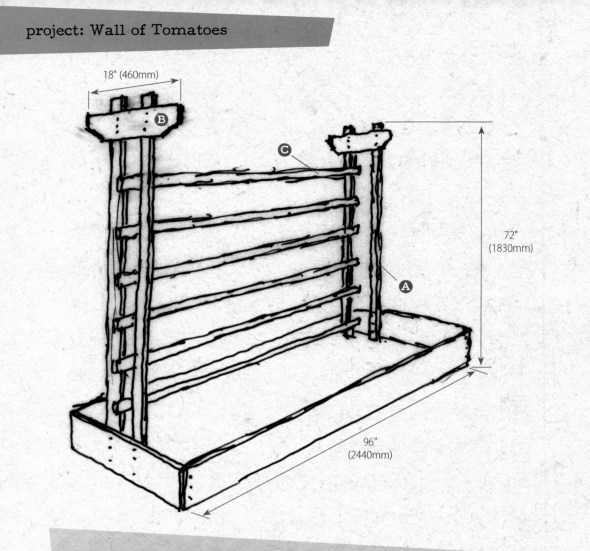

18" (460mm)

72" (1830mm)

96" (2440mm)

WALL OF TOMATOES MATERIALS LIST

item	material	dimensions	quantity
A Vertical posts	2x2 (38 x 38mm)	72" (1830mm)	4
B Top rails	1x4 (19 x 89mm)	18" (460mm)	4
C Horizontal strips	1x2 (19 x 38mm) halved along the length	96" (2440mm)	6
Deck screws		3" (75mm)	

TOMATO VARIETIES

There are two main types of tomato: determinate and indeterminate. Basically, determinate types form flowers at the terminal growing point, which stops growth and keeps the plant at a certain height. Indeterminate types don't do this, and so will continue to grow taller throughout the season. For the tomato wall, you want indeterminate tomato plants. Try these popular indeterminate varieties.

name	average fruit size	days to maturity	notes
Amish Paste	5–7 oz	82 days	All-purpose tomato
Better Boy	12 oz	72 days	Great for slicing
Big Beef	16 oz	73 days	Large meaty fruit
Early Girl	5 oz	54 days	First tomatoes of the season
Georgia Streak	16–32 oz	90 days	Yellow with red streaks
Mortgage Lifter	32 oz	79 days	One of the largest tomato varieties
Mountain Gold	8 oz	70 days	Orange color
Super Sweet 100	1 inch (25mm) diameter	70 days	Cherry tomatoes
Sweet Million	1 inch (25mm) diameter	65 days	Crack-resistant cherry tomatoes
Yellow Pear	2 inches (50mm) long	80 days	Pear-shaped with a sweet flavor

Biologically speaking, tomatoes are fruit, although they are referred to as vegetables in the culinary world.

1

1 Make the sides. This trellis has two identical side panels that consist of two vertical posts (A) and a pair of upper rails (B). I cut a decorative profile on the upper rail (B) just to make it a bit more interesting. These parts were fastened together by screws. To make the second side, I used the first as a template. This ensures that they go together identically, so even if they're slightly out of square, at least they'll be consistent to each other.

2 Secure the sides. I attached the vertical posts (A) to the sides of one of our raised beds with 3" (75mm) deck screws. At this point, you could also drive the sides down into your garden plot if desired.

2

3 **Add the horizontal pieces.** I used a level to get the horizontal strips (C) lined up properly; then, I nailed the horizontal strips to the support posts with a nailer (though screws would be a good choice, too).

4 **Train the tomatoes.** Here's the completed trellis. This early in the season, the plants barely reach the bottom strip, but that changed as the season went on. To keep the plants growing upwards, I wove the stems between the horizontal strips as they grew, but you can also use string or wire to fasten wayward stems as needed. This probably won't be necessary, but if you tie up the plants, make sure that you make big enough loops so that the plant has room to grow without being choked later on. In the last photo, the plants are over 5' (1525mm) tall, and it was only early July. I actually had to add on another horizontal strip higher up.

You can enjoy the tomatoes off your vines as much as you want, but don't eat the leaves; they're toxic!

WALL OF TOMATOES #2

Here's the second wall of tomatoes: it is an anchored trellis, meaning that it is attached to another structural element. In this case, it is screwed to the sides of a raised bed. For infill material, I used plastic poultry netting, since it is very inexpensive and seemed like it would work fine. I fastened it to the vertical supports with staples. Because poultry netting comes in 36" (915mm)-wide rolls, you will need two swathes to cover the entire trellis.

WALL OF TOMATOES #2 MATERIALS LIST

item	material	dimensions	qty.
Vertical posts	2x2 (38 x 38mm)	84" (2135mm)	2
Horizontal rail	2x2 (38 x 38mm)	96" (2440mm)	1
Infill	Plastic netting	100" x 36" (2540 x 915mm)	2

Other Materials That Can Be Used For Trellis Infill

- ❏ Chicken wire
- ❏ Dog-fencing (rectangular) wire
- ❏ Concrete mesh
- ❏ Twine (vertical or horizontal)
- ❏ Pre-woven grids
- ❏ Lattice
- ❏ Wire (spooled)

WALL OF TOMATOES #3

This trellis is freestanding. You often see trellises like this built with A-frame sides, but in this instance, the tomatoes were located too close to the fence for this to work out—poor planning on my part. I got around this misstep by running the rear legs of the trellis vertically. I filled into the middle of the trellis with poultry netting.

WALL OF TOMATOES #3 MATERIALS LIST

item	material	dimensions	qty.
Vertical posts	2x2 (38 x 38mm)	84" (2135mm)	2
Horizontal rail	2x2 (38 x 38mm)	96" (2440mm)	1
Diagonal braces	2x2 (38 x 38mm)	120" (3050mm)	2
Infill	Plastic netting	100" x 36" (2540 x 915mm)	2

China produces more tomatoes than any other country in the world.

BEAN LEANER

An Easy-To-Move Design For Your Beans To Climb

Trellises, at least in my mind, come in two forms: those that are free-standing, and those that require some other kind of support. This particular trellis belongs to the latter group, in that I designed it to be leaned up against whatever else is around. Originally, I had placed it against a fence, but it turned out that I didn't need it there, because the beans that I had planted in that spot were bush beans instead of pole beans. I guess I did a pretty bad job of reading the seed package! In any event, it was no problem to move the trellis to a different bed where I was getting ready to plant more beans. The second time around, I was much more careful about checking the label. And leaning trellises aren't just useful when you need to correct a silly mistake: they are really handy because they can be moved around from year to year. Since they have no moving parts, they're easy to set up, take down, and store during the off-season.

BEAN VARIETIES

Since you're already hard at work building a support structure for your bean plants, here's a list of the different varieties you can grow when you're finished:

name	vine size	days to maturity	notes
Blue Lake Pole	6'–7' (1829–2134mm)	70 days	Use in soups or freeze and can
Genuine Cornfield	5'–6' (1524–1829mm)	70–90 days	Often grown in cornfields
King of the Garden Pole Lima	8' (2438mm)	90 days	Large beans with a sweet flavor
Old Homestead Pole Bean (Kentucky Wonder)	More than 6' (1829mm)	70 days	Variety from the 1860s
Romano Pole Bean	6' (1829mm)	70 days	Harvest pods often
Scarlet Runner Pole Bean	10' (3048mm)	70 days	Vines have bright red flowers

Beans are warm-weather vegetables and should not be planted until all signs of frost have left your region.

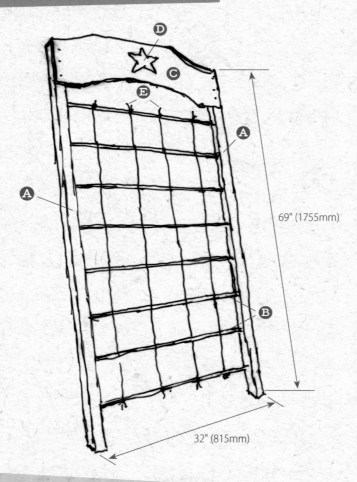

69" (1755mm)

32" (815mm)

BEAN LEANER MATERIALS LIST

	item	material	dimensions	quantity
A	Posts	2x2 (38 x 38mm)	66" (1675mm)	2
B	Horizontal supports	7⁄16" (11mm) dowel rods	30"	8
C	Top rail	¼" (6mm) plywood	32" x 9" (815 x 230mm)	1
D	Star decoration	Scrap wood	Size as desired	1
E	Vertical supports	Nylon string		

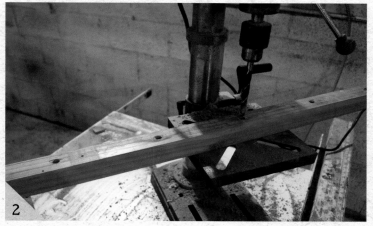

1 Cut the posts. Since this trellis is basically a large rectangle that gets most of its strength from its two vertical posts, that's where I started. I ripped a 2x4 (38 x 89mm) in half on my table saw to produce the posts (A), and then I set them next to each other on a pair of sawhorses to lay out a series of marks where the horizontal rods would be placed. The easiest way to do this is to start in the middle and keep dividing each length about in half until you have as many marks as you want rods—an even number is easiest. I picked eight.

2 Drill holes. To ensure that the holes for the rods (B) were drilled exactly perpendicular to the surface of the posts (A), I used my drill press. You could definitely use a hand drill in a pinch, but the drill press does help to make certain that the rods will line up neatly later on. Make sure the holes you drill are the same size as the diameter of the dowels you're using.

Wet beans can deteriorate very quickly, so wash your beans right before you cook them, rather than before refrigerator storage.

SQUASH RAMP
Corral Your Favorite Sprawling Squashes and Melons

This is a fun structure a lot like Wall of Tomatoes #2 (page 88). Zucchini, cucumbers, and squash plants sprawl endlessly and take up a lot of real estate—so my goal was to reduce the footprint of these plants in the garden. The ramp worked pretty well to limit this, and also to keep the plants up off the ground so they didn't harbor moisture and become a breeding ground for bugs and other pests.

Because we have some raised beds, I knew I could anchor the vertical posts to the sides of the bed, and that greatly simplified the design. Instead of orienting the ramp straight up and down, I leaned it back at an angle so the heavy vegetables have some support under them. I used 2" (50mm) wood screws to secure the bottoms of the posts to the edges of the raised beds.

I used thick plastic netting as an infill between the posts, and this ended up being a good choice: the sturdy mesh provided a strong substrate that never sagged.

You can join the corners of the frame any way you'd like. In this case, I spent a couple of minutes cutting out some decorative and functional braces from ¼" (6mm)-thick scrap plywood. I then screwed them directly to the vertical posts and the horizontal top rail—easy as pie.

⭐ VINE VEGETABLE VARIETIES

If you have the space (and with the help of this project, you will), there are lots of vine fruits and vegetables you can grow in your backyard. Here are some favorite vine plant varieties that you can explore:

name	season	size	notes
Fastbreak Cantaloupe	Summer (May)	4–5 lb. (about 2kg)	Classic orange flesh
Hearts of Gold Cantaloupe	Summer (May)	3 lb. (1kg)	Sweet, thick flesh
County Fair Cucumber	Spring (after last frost)	3" (76mm)	Great for pickling
Slice Master Cucumber	Spring (after last frost)	8"–9" (200–230mm)	Good for container gardening
Honey Pearl Honeydew	Summer (May)	4–8 lb. (2–4kg)	Texture similar to Asian pears
Honey Orange Honeydew	Summer (May)	3 lb. (1kg)	Crisp, orange flesh
Casper Pumpkin	Winter (August–September)	12"–18" (305–457mm) tall; 10–15 lb. (5–7kg)	Sweet flesh is great for pies
Sugar Pie Pumpkin	Winter (August–September)	7"–8" (178–203mm) diameter	Good for carving, painting, or cooking
Butternut Squash	Winter (August–September)	8"–13" (203–330mm) long, 3"–7" (76–178mm) wide	One of the most popular for culinary purposes
Spaghetti Squash	Winter (August–September)	8"–9" (203–229mm) long, 4"–5" (102–127mm) wide	Great pasta substitute
Globe Zucchini	Summer (May–August)	Softball size; 3" (76mm) diameter	Great for stuffing
Golden Zucchini	Summer (May–August)	Best at 6"–8" (152–203mm)	Bright yellow skin

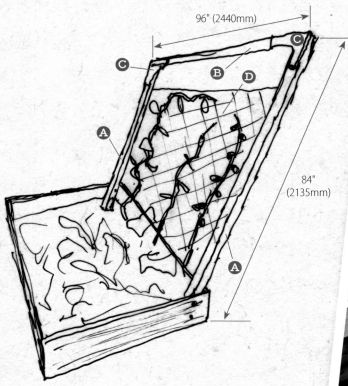

96" (2440mm)

84" (2135mm)

SQUASH RAMP
MATERIALS LIST

	item	material	dimensions	quantity
A	Vertical posts	2x2 (38 x 38mm)	84" (2135mm)	2
B	Horizontal top rail	2x2 (38 x 38mm)	96" (2440mm)	1
C	Corner braces	¼" (6mm) plywood	10" x 10" (255 x 255mm)	2
D	Infill	Poultry netting	100" x 36" (2540 x 915mm)	2
	Screws	2" (50mm)		

Squash varieties are some of the world's oldest crops; several date back 10,000 years.

GRAPEVINE LADDER
Sturdy Ladder Design Looks Good With Or Without Grapes

I am hardly the most ambitious backyard farmer I know—not even close!—but no matter where you fit in along the continuum from novice to experienced full-timer, there is always more to learn. That's half the fun! I get incredible amounts of satisfaction from growing new things and finding novel ways to do so. This year, I decided to try my hand at growing grapes. I have a lot of friends who have grapes in their yards, and I've always wanted my own so I could make juice and wine. Also, the vines themselves are so big that they can become a kind of architectural element and help to define an area of a backyard in a really cool way.

A quick trip to our local garden center set me up with three plants that seemed like a good match for both our climate and my intentions, and then it was time to build a trellis. My friend Jimmy, a master gardener if ever there was one, picked out the spot for me based on its exposure to the sun and its compatibility with the way our yard is set up. Our backyard has a large deck that is raised about 6" (150mm) off the ground,

and the deck bumps up against a large outbuilding where I have an office. Jimmy assured me this was a prime location, so I cut back the deck boards in three spots and planned out a simple trellis system that would support the vines as they grow and add some visual interest in the meantime.

Bear in mind that mature grapevines can be quite heavy, so whatever you build will need to be sturdy. In this case, I was glad I could anchor the trellis to the exterior wall of an outbuilding. You're certainly not limited to this approach— freestanding grapevine trellises are standard issue everywhere grapes are grown—but this setup worked best for our needs.

When you're planting new grapevines, be aware that a tidy approach will help out during the first year. Left to their own devices, grapevines will tend to sprawl all over the place, but you should actually trim back any random offshoots so you have a healthy cane you can train upward on the trellis.

There are close to 25 million acres of grapes throughout the world, and one acre yields about 15,000 glasses of wine.

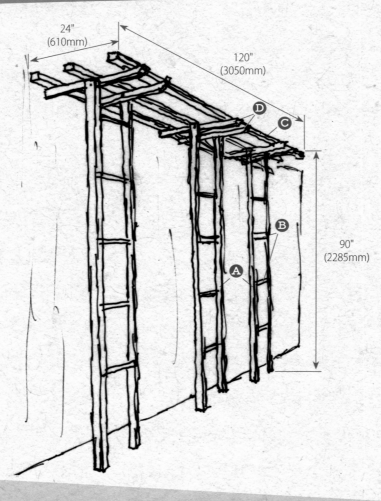

GRAPEVINE LADDER MATERIALS LIST

item	material	dimensions	quantity
A Ladder posts	2x2 (38 x 38mm) (I cut mine from 2x4s [38 x 89mm])	90" (2285mm)	6
B Ladder rungs	¾" x ⅝" (19 x 16mm) or whatever is handy	16" (405mm)	15
C Spanners	2x2 (38 x 38mm) (I cut mine from 2x4s [38 x 89mm])	120" (3050mm)	3
D Top supports	2x2 (38 x 38mm)	24" (610mm)	6
1½" (38mm) brad nails			
2½" (65mm) screws			

1 Cut the notches for the ladder rungs.

The heart of this design is the ladder-like vertical components (A) that the grapevines will wrap around as they head for the upper horizontal section. You could fabricate the ladders in any number of ways, but here's how I did it. I used a dado blade on my table saw, in conjunction with a miter gauge, to cut a series of notches spaced 15" (380mm) apart in the 2x4s (A). The notches are ¾" (19mm) wide and ⅝" (16mm) deep. If you use another size of lumber for ladder rungs (B), be sure to match the size of the notches to it.

2 Rip the 2x4s for the ladder posts.

Once the notches are cut, I switched back to a normal blade and ripped the 2x4s in half to create the ladder posts (A). I needed six 2x2s, so I started with three 2x4s. The reason I cut the notches prior to ripping is that it is faster than vice versa—cutting the notches was a slower process, after all. While you're at it, rip the spanners (C), and also the top supports (D) if you're making them from 2x4s. Because I'm installing my trellis on a building, I wanted one end of each support (D) to be square—the other has an angled cut, as you can see in the photos. If you're creating a freestanding trellis, you will probably want all the support ends to match.

For those of you watching calories, grapes are 80 percent water, making them a great snack food.

3 **Set the rungs.** When the vertical posts (A) were done, my daughter and I set in the rungs (B). They were a pretty tight fit, which is a good thing. We pounded them in with a rubber mallet and then tacked them with 1½" (38mm) brad nails.

4 **Put the ladders in place.** This photo shows the trellis as a whole beginning to shape up. The bases of the ladders were 12" (305mm) from the wall.

If you're not installing your grapevine trellis on a building like I did, then the best way to do the next few steps is to lay the ladders flat on the ground, spaced evenly over a 10' (3050mm) span.

3

4

5 **Install the first spanner.** When I had tentatively placed the ladders, I affixed one of the long spanners (C) to the wall using a nail gun. A level is a necessary tool for getting it properly aligned. I readjusted the ladders so there was about 8" (205mm) of spanner overhanging on each end—do what looks good to you.

If you're creating a freestanding trellis, just lay one of the spanners (C) underneath the very top of the ladders. Adjust it until the spacing looks good; mark the location of the inside of each ladder post (A) on the spanner (C). Don't attach the spanner yet.

6 **Install one set of top supports.** Having the rear spanner (C) in place allowed me to attach the short horizontal pieces (D) that run front-to-back. These top support pieces (D) go underneath the spanner (C) and inside the ladder posts (A). I countersunk long 2½" (65mm) screws to join the parts together.

To make a freestanding version, first attach one pair of top supports (D) to the ladder posts (A). Make sure the ladder is centered on the supports. Installation is easiest if you flip the ladder so the inside of one post is facing upward as you attach the support to that side. When both supports are attached to the ladder, align the outsides of the supports (D) with the marks you made on the spanner in Step 5. Front-to-back, position the pieces so the spanner (C) is in a bit from the ends of the supports (D).

It takes about 2½ lb. (1kg) of grapes to make a quality bottle of wine.

7

7 Install the rest of the top supports.
To make sure that the long horizontal spanners (C) would line up properly, I used a level to put on the other sets of top supports (D).

For the freestanding version, continue by installing the other two sets of top supports (D). When you're done, the ladders will be attached to the supports (D), and the supports will be attached to the first spanner (C).

8 Install the last two spanners.
Position the middle spanner right in front of the ladder posts (A), and the final spanner a few inches from the end of the top supports (D). Attach with screws or nails.

If you built a freestanding trellis, take it to the site where you want it installed, dig a trench, and bury the ladders up to the first rung. The whole project will be sturdier if you build two sets and attach them with some more 2x2s to make an arbor. The trellis is finished—time to play the waiting game while the grapevines catch up.

8

GRAPE VARIETIES

Grapes are a versatile plant that can be used to stock your kitchen with delicious jelly and juice. They are perfect as a low calorie snack and can be used to make your own wine. Give these varieties a try:

name	growing conditions	color	notes
Bluebell	Can survive in cooler conditions	Blue-black	Best for making juice or jelly
Concord Seedless	Can survive in cooler conditions	Blue-black	Good for fresh eating, juice, or jelly
Edelweiss	Can survive in cooler conditions	White	Good on its own, or for wine, juice, or jelly
Glenora	Best in warmer conditions	Blue-black	Eat these fresh off the vine
Golden Muscat	Cool conditions	White grape	Primarily used for wine production
Vanessa	Cool conditions	Red	Best for eating

HOP VARIETIES

If you're growing grapes for the purpose of making your own wine, you also might want to consider growing a few hop plants to brew your own beer. Here are some popular hop varieties you can incorporate into your garden:

name	purpose	beer type	characteristics
Centennial	Aroma	American ales	Creates a bitter flavor and sometimes adds a citrus or floral taste
Chinook	Bittering	American pale ales	Adds a smoky note
Fuggle	Aroma	English-style ales; lagers	Mild floral or grassy aroma
Golding	Aroma	Ales; lagers; stouts; bitters	Imparts a spicy flavor and aroma
Hallertau	Aroma	Lagers; pilsners	Adds a spicy flavor and aroma
Saaz	Bittering	Pilsners; lagers	Clean, bitter flavor

A grapevine can grow up to 50' (15m) in length.

1 **Prep the materials.** Constructing a trellis like this is pretty simple. Grab some 2x4 and rip it into three, or a 2x2 and rip it in half. As a starting point, figure out how tall the plant you're using the trellis for is going to grow. We planted Alaska peas, which grow to about 3' (915mm) tall, so that determined the height of our trellis. Cut four side pieces (A) that are about 12" (305mm) longer than your plant's eventual height. The top and bottom support pieces (from the same wood) (B) could be whatever size you want—I used about 22" (560mm)-long pieces.

2 **Add chicken wire.** Lay out two side pieces (A) about as far apart as the width you want. Chicken wire (C) is a little tricky to work with, so you may want to wear gloves to protect you from its sharp ends. It is easily cut with either tin snips or, as I'm using here, wire cutters. Cut the wire so it fits comfortably over the pieces. Staple down the wire onto the side pieces (A) and trim any extra.

3 **Complete the frame.** Nail the top and bottom pieces (B) onto the assembly. Note that I left 6" (150mm) of the long supports protruding below the chicken wire so I would have a place to attach the frame to the container.

4 **Make a second frame.** Repeat Steps 2 and 3 to create a second frame.

2

3

4

5

5 Assemble the trellis. I used 1½" (40mm) screws to secure the frames in place. Make sure to predrill the holes so the thin support pieces don't crack. Connect the sides with a horizontal piece (D) at the top of the structure. This added some strength to the side frames, and it provided a place to tie some strings, weighted with large washers, that I could run down for the pea plants to climb up. If you're building the trellis as a freestanding piece, put more pieces (D) at the top and bottom of both sides to connect the frames.

PEA VARIETIES

If you'd like to explore the different varieties of peas available, consider purchasing a seed packet containing seeds for several plants. Many garden companies sell these packets, and they're a great way to find a new garden favorite. While you're experimenting, consider giving some of these varieties a try:

name	category	days to maturity	notes
Avalanche	Snow	60 days	Large 6" (152mm)-long pods
Little Marvel	Garden	65 days	Produces sweet, tender peas
Mr. Big	Garden	60 days	Produces extra-large peas
Snowbird	Snow	60 days	Short plant, averaging 18" (457mm) tall
Spring	Garden	60 days	Produces lots of pods with 6–7 peas per pod
Sugar Bon	Snap	55 days	Extra sweet pods
Sugar Daddy	Snow	75 days	Sweet, tender pods
Sugar Snap	Snap	65 days	Traditional snap pea variety
Super Snappy	Snap	60 days	Available only from Burpee Seed Company

In 1984, Janet Harris ate 7,175 peas one by one using chopsticks; she holds the world record.

OPEN SEASON
Growing Season Extenders

Although some parts of the country have weather that allows residents to garden year-round, most of us aren't so lucky. It is pretty easy, however, to extend the season at least a little bit and enjoy fresh produce for longer than you might expect. For example, Lynsey Gammon, an urban farmer who is profiled in this book (page 112), grows lettuces all winter long using a simple cloche. Other season extenders include cold frames and greenhouses, both of which are covered in this section.

LYNSEY GAMMON
Salt Lake City, Utah

Lynsey is an energetic backyard farmer who is putting in a lot of hard work as she inches closer to her dream: a two or three acre farm in the country with a large diversity of food crops. What she has already accomplished is inspiring, and I have no doubt that she'll end up right where she wants to be. In the meantime, she is learning a ton and providing food on a regular basis for 25–30 people. She is also working on the legal and structural end of setting up a business—charmingly named Roots and Boots—that will take her venture to another level. She has also begun selling produce at a downtown store that spotlights local growers, and as an added bonus, she provides recipes to her clients to help them get the most out of her harvest.

maintaining a balance

Her story began six years ago when Lynsey and her husband, Dan, started growing food in their yard. They have a great setup with trellises, mini hoop houses, and the tallest pea plants I've ever seen. Every year they undertake a new project, such as ripping out some water-hungry grass and replacing it with another raised bed for vegetable production. She notes that there is a tricky balance to maintain, however, since a certain amount of open space is rather nice to have for her two-year old daughter, Hazel, to play on. This year, they've added a chicken coop to their yard, which will be fun for the whole family and a great source of both eggs and compost.

Although she has risen to the challenges of farming, Lynsey didn't have a background in it. Her success demonstrates just what is possible when you're motivated and put in the time to learn a new set of skills. She has a master's degree in Public Health from the University of Utah, and she worked in the field of women's health for a while. After Hazel was born, Lynsey was ready for a change. It seemed only natural at that point to delve into farming, and so she read every book she could find on the subject. She also took an Introduction to Horticulture class to brush up on the basics.

⬆ Lynsey Gammon grows enough food in her backyard (and others) to feed 25 to 30 people.

🔧 Grass needs about 1" (25mm) of water each week.

By now, farming has turned into a full-time commitment. This is evident in the fact that Lynsey has seen a better and better crop every year, and she's gained a ton of knowledge along the way. She is modest about her achievements, but perhaps this is because she has her eye on the future: Lynsey's goal is for farming to become a viable business someday.

finding space

The hardest part for her has been finding and managing space. Although she is able to produce quite a bit from her own yard, she has needed to branch out in order to increase her yields. To meet this challenge, she has entered into a yard-sharing partnership with a friend, and this has worked out pretty well all around. The essence of the arrangement is that Lynsey does the work to transform a neglected lot into a beautiful and healthy garden, and the landowner gets unlimited free produce. In this cash-free deal, everybody comes out ahead. Lynsey is always on the lookout for other plots, with a special interest in those that are close to home to keep things simple and efficient. This fall, she is planning on cultivating cold weather crops in some other yards.

This massive raised bed produces a ton of food. Lynsey rotates crops to maximize her harvests, and the beds are equipped with a useful drip irrigation system that saves both water and time.

The straw mulch beneath these tomato plants helps to limit weed growth and slow the rate at which water evaporates from the soil.

I was totally jealous of Lynsey's pea plants. I thought mine were doing well, but then I saw hers and was thoroughly humbled.

growing year-round

I was impressed with Lynsey's ability to grow year-round in a place with some pretty tough winters. Lynsey and Dan grew delicious greens—spinach, arugula, and kale—all winter long thanks to a cold frame positioned in their south-facing front yard. Managing the temperature took a bit of time—they placed a thermometer inside to help—and on the coldest nights, they ran a string of Christmas lights inside to provide a bit of heat. I thought this was a great idea, and I plan to copy their idea this winter myself.

Lynsey also commented on the high levels of support she is seeing for locally-grown food in her area: she feels like she is pretty much in the right place at the right time. Where some cities have enjoyed a robust—and therefore intensely competitive—local food movement for a while now, the trend is newer in Salt Lake City. This provides more opportunities for start-ups like hers. Given her enthusiasm, her commitment, and her willingness to work hard over the long term, I have no doubt that Lynsey will continue her success. She is clearly having a great time along the way, and that is impressive in its own right.

By tying some lengths of bamboo fencing into tubes, Lynsey created some really effective and neat-looking potato planters. You can see some shoots poking their way out the sides.

Charles Darwin's study of the pea vine can be found in *The Movement and Habits of Climbing Plants*.

GREENHOUSE
Recycled Windows Make This An Easy-To-Customize Doubly Green Project

This was a super-fun project I built in conjunction with two of my favorite backyard farmers, Kevin and Jael. They had a huge yard, and it seems like nearly every square inch of it is producing food. They have a bunch of fruit trees, chickens (which they raise for meat and eggs), grapevines, and a huge garden for fresh produce.

They recently had the windows replaced on their house, and Kevin, ever the resourceful guy, stockpiled them for a project just such as this. They also scavenged a few from one of Jael's colleagues, and so we had quite a nice assortment to choose from. While I think you can adapt this greenhouse design to just about whatever size windows you happen to come across, it was nice to have a lot so that we had some flexibility in which ones we used and where we placed them. That is really the first step in the process: taking stock of what you have to work with, and reconciling that with your rough conception of how large a footprint you'd like to take up. Kevin and Jael had plenty of wiggle room in the spot they chose, but they figured that an 80" x 60" (2000 x 1500mm) floor plan would be

ideal, so we sorted through the piles of windows with this in mind. The 80" x 60" dimension was also based largely on the fact that they had a pair of old patio doors that, when used in tandem, could provide a nice roof for the structure.

Because Kevin and Jael were able to find used windows for the project, this is truly a greenhouse in more ways than one. We estimated that 80% of the materials were reclaimed or recycled. Doing this makes sense from every perspective: it kept a pile of perfectly good windows out of the landfill, it gave us all a real feeling of satisfaction, and it saved money. The total bill for this project came in at under $100, which all went toward the lumber. If you can get your hands on some used 2x4s, you'll save even more.

If you're looking for a place to find used building materials, I have two good tips. Online classifieds—which includes places like Craigslist—often have quite a lot to offer. In addition, many cities have stores that focus on reselling old building materials to the public. The Habitat for Humanity operates ReStores in our city, and I recommend them highly.

Cornwall, England, houses the world's largest greenhouse, known as Eden Project.

GREENHOUSE MATERIALS LIST

item	materials	dimensions	quantity
Nails			
Screws			
Latches for transoms			

Rear Wall

	item	materials	dimensions	quantity
RA	King studs	2x4 (38 x 89mm)	96" (2440mm)	2
RB	Top and bottom plates	2x4 (38 x 89mm)	75" (1905mm)	2
RC	Studs	2x4 (38 x 89mm)	92⅝" (2353mm)	3
RD	Panels	½" (11mm) plywood 78" x 48" (1980 x 1220mm)		2

Side Walls (Makes 2)

	item	materials	dimensions	quantity
SA	Tall king studs	2x4 (38 x 89mm)	96" (2440mm)	2
SB	Short king studs	2x4 (38 x 89mm)	72" (1830mm)	2
SC	Studs	2x4 (38 x 89mm)	84" (2135mm)	4
SD	Top and bottom plates	2x4 (38 x 89mm)	53" (1345mm)	4
SE	Windows		36" x 28" (915 x 710mm)	8
SF	Door hinges			4
SG	¼" (6mm) translucent plastic panels		58" x 27½" (1475 x 700mm)	4

Front Wall

	item	materials	dimensions	quantity
FA	King studs	2x4 (38 x 89mm)	72" (1830mm)	2
FB	Studs	2x4 (38 x 89mm)	55" (1400mm)	2
FC	Top and bottom plates	2x4 (38 x 89mm)	63" (1600mm)	2
FD	Tall windows		58" x 22" (1475 x 560mm)	3
FE	Transom windows		32" x 14" (815 x 355mm)	2
FF	Hinges		Any size	4
FG	Filler	2x4 (38 x 89mm) and plywood as needed	To fit	

Roof

	item	materials	dimensions	quantity
RFA	Patio doors		80"x 40" (2030 x 1015mm)	2
RFB	Roof supports	2x4 (38 x 89mm)	60" (1525mm)	4

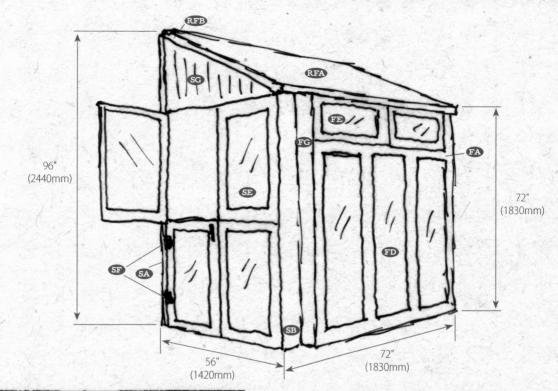

96"
(2440mm)

72"
(1830mm)

56"
(1420mm)

72"
(1830mm)

RFB

RFA

SG

FE

FG

FA

SE

FD

SF   SA

SB

1 **Select a site.** When siting a greenhouse, you'll naturally want to take into account the best location for making the most of limited daylight in the winter. This means finding a good southern exposure, ideally. In this case, the greenhouse actually faced west, which still gets a ton of sunlight in the afternoon. Because the roof of the greenhouse is glass, we knew that it would be able to pick up a lot of light throughout the day anyway. The overall orientation of the greenhouse should provide plenty of light and heat, and it allowed us to tuck the structure up against a fence in a way that worked best for the yard overall. If the site isn't already cleared out and basically flat, you'll want to start there. Kevin prepped the spot with a shovel and a rake.

Greenhouses were used in sixteenth century France to grow tropical plants with medicinal qualities.

2 Review the window selection.
You should begin by making a list of the windows you have on hand. Make a note of both their quantity and dimensions. If you have more than one of a particular size, that can come in handy when it comes time to stack them on top of each other; it is easy to make sure the 2x4 (38 x 89mm) framing is in the right place when the vertical edges of the windows line up. The materials list shows the windows used for this project to give you a general guideline—but keep in mind that you don't need those exact window sizes. Apply this building process to the selection you have to make a unique greenhouse.

3 Construct the rear wall. The concept behind the construction was fairly straightforward: simple walls framed with 2x4s would form a skeleton to which the windows could be attached by screwing through their frames. We assembled the rear wall on a flat spot near the site. You want a king stud (RA) (so called because it spans from the very top of the wall to the very bottom) on both ends of the wall. A top and bottom plate (RB) complete the rectangle; then, three studs (RC) are spaced evenly inside the rectangle. After you have everything laid out, attach the pieces with two nails or screws into the end grain of each piece of lumber.

2

3

4 Make sure the rear wall is square. To make sure the finished greenhouse would look right, all of the individual components had to be straight, flat, and square. To square a large assembly like the rear wall, you can simply measure the diagonals. If they're not exactly the same length, shift the frame slightly until they are.

5 Nail plywood to the outer rectangle. We also wanted to make sure the structure was really sturdy, so we decided to make the rear wall solid, sheathed in plywood. We hoped that this would lend rigidity to the greenhouse as a whole, and it worked out great. We used a nail gun to affix the plywood sheeting (RD), but a good old-fashioned hammer will work fine, too. Building codes generally require nails every 6" (150mm) along the periphery in this kind of application. We didn't conform exactly to that, but it isn't a bad guideline to keep in mind.

6 Nail plywood to the center studs. To be able to sink nails into the studs in the center, we just drew lines across the panel. This is much easier than trying to estimate by eye, which will invariably be off a bit. Again, as a guideline, building codes generally require nails every 12" (305mm) in the center of a panel.

Many of today's commercial greenhouses are using geothermal systems to heat their structures.

7 Raise the rear wall. Once the rear wall was sheathed, we set it into place (plywood side outward) and held it upright with a temporary brace—a 2x4 set on angle and nailed to the wall.

8 Mock up a side wall. With the rear wall in place, it was much easier to start to imagine how the rest of the construction would proceed. We decided to build one of the side walls next, so we laid out a 2x4 to indicate the bottom of the wall, and we set a couple of windows into place so that we could see how far out the wall might extend. This photo shows Kevin using a tape measure to get a sense for the slope of the roof.

9 Construct one side wall. Our mockup of the wall helped us to establish that it should slope from 96" (2440mm) high at the back to 72" (1830mm) at the front. We cut 2x4s to these lengths (SA, SB) and nailed them to a shorter length of 2x4 (SD) that would run across the bottom of the wall. The ends of the top 2x4 (SD) needed to be cut at an angle, and this was easy to handle: we just set a 2x4 (SD) into place and marked it directly from the vertical pieces (SA, SB). We didn't need to know the measurement of the angle or do any math—cutting on the line made for a perfect fit. We also added a pair of 2x4s (SC) (doubled up for strength) to the center of the wall at the place where the windows butted up against each other.

**building projects for the
BACKYARD FARMER**

10 **Attach the side wall to the rear wall.** After nailing the side wall into the vertical stud at the corner of the rear wall, the emerging structure began to feel a bit more substantial.

11 **Attach the windows to the side wall.** Attaching the windows (SE) to the frame was simple—we just screwed them directly onto the 2x4s. We started with the bottom windows and worked our way up from there. There was no way to tell how far the glass extended into the window's frame, so we just tried to keep the screws toward the outside edges. This seemed to work, because we didn't hit a single pane. The holes needed to be pre-drilled in order to minimize the stress on the windows.

12 **Construct the front wall.** Lay out the two king studs (FA), the top and bottom plates (FC), and the doubled-up studs (FB). Nail everything together. Raise the frame and attach it to the side wall already in place. As we worked, we tried to mentally stay a step ahead by keeping in mind the dimensions of the windows we had to work with. This led us to realize we had three 58" x 22" (1475 x 560mm) windows (FD) that made for a nice bottom course, and that we could top them with a pair of transom windows (FE) that measured 32" x 14" (815 x 355mm). This meant the windows all lined up almost perfectly, which was partially just luck, but I'd like to think being creative had a little bit to do with it as well. Nail on the bottom course of windows (FD).

Favorite greenhouse crops include tomatoes, peppers, and cucumbers.

13 **Install the transoms.** In order to regulate temperature and humidity inside the greenhouse, we wanted the transom windows (FE) to be operable. My first instinct was to hinge them at the top, but I quickly nixed this because that would've meant we'd have to come up with a way to prop them open; putting the hinges (FF) on the bottom solved this problem. Install a simple latch at the top of each window to keep them shut when closed.

14 **Fill in the gaps.** Because of the size of the windows we had to work with, the overall length of the front wall was 10½" (270mm) narrower than the rear wall. If we had had a couple of really skinny windows, we would've worked them in, but instead we just made a spacer from 2x4s and plywood (FG) that built out the front wall to the required length. There was also a small 2" (50mm) gap between the transom windows (FE). We dealt with this by installing a 2x4 (FG) behind the gap.

13

14

15

16

15 Construct the final side wall.
Construct, attach, and window the final side wall as you did in Steps 9–11. The final wall needed to accommodate a doorway. To keep the wall rigid, we framed its bottom edge in with a 2x4. We positioned the doorway at the back of the side wall. You could install the door windows now, but we waited until after the roof was on.

16 Fill in the eaves. Kevin, ever a resourceful individual, had been saving an old sheet of ¼" (6mm) translucent plastic, and we used this to create panels (SG) that would fill in the space below the eaves. Unless you have a flat roof, which would seem likely to create drainage issues, you'll probably have to do something like this with most greenhouses, whether they have gabled or shed-style roofs. And talk about designing as you go: we realized that, in order for the transom windows to have enough room to open and close, we would need to raise the roof up a bit. We opted to elevate it 3½" (89mm), which is the width of a 2x4 turned on edge, which is why the panel extends beyond the 2x4 in this picture.

Take temperature readings in your greenhouse every few days; you'll learn what types of plants you can grow during different seasons.

17

17 Install the roof. Attach four 2x4s (RFB) to support the roof. There should be one on both sides (these should be on edge). Install one down the middle so it matches the pitch of the two side top plates (SD). Put the last roof support (RFB) on edge on top of this middle spanner. We used a set of old double-glazed patio doors (RFA) for the roof. They have an extremely strong metal frame, which we screwed through to fix them in place.

18 Install the door. We had picked out a pair of 28" (710mm)-wide windows to make into a door, but when it came time to put them together, we realized that we didn't even need to: by hanging them independently with sturdy door hinges (SF), we created a Dutch door that is kind of cute, and has no functional downside. A pair of shop-made handles makes them easy to open and close.

18

You can use mulch to create your greenhouse floor, and then plant vegetables straight in the ground.

COLD FRAME
Quick Project Extends Growing Season and Hardens-Off Early Spring Seedlings

Want to extend your growing season? Cold frames are a great way to do just that. Their clear tops allow sunlight to enter, and they keep heat in, especially during the night. Historically, cold frames were built in addition to a heated greenhouse. The name exemplifies the distinction between the warm greenhouse and the unheated cold frame. They were frequently built as part of the greenhouse's foundation brickwork along the southern wall (in northern latitudes). This allowed seeds to be germinated in the greenhouse and then easily moved to the attached cold frame to be hardened-off before final planting outside. It is also possible to use cold frames year-round—just keep the lid open during the summer, and then close it up again to keep lettuces and other plants growing all winter long. As the season advances, you'll want to make sure to open the windows on sunny days so that your plants don't fry in the heat of the sun and the reflection of the glass windows.

I spoke with a guy recently who had a bad experience using old windows for a cold frame—he remarked that glass isn't shatter-proof, and one of his panes had broken, which caused a messy cascade of shards to fall into the soil below. From then on, he's used plastic, since it is much less likely to break, and if it does, it won't cause much of a mess.

COLD FRAME MATERIALS LIST

The dimensions for this cold frame were determined by the size of an old window I had lying around. It measured 70" x 24" (1780 x 610mm). Apply this building process to whatever materials you have available, or whatever end size you desire. You'll also want a stick to prop open the lid on warm days so the plants don't overheat.

item	materials	dimensions	qty.
Ⓐ End panels	¾" (17mm) plywood	21" high x 18" deep (530 x 460mm)	2
Ⓑ Front and back	2x4 (38 x 89mm)	68" (1730mm)	9
Ⓒ Lid	Old window	70" x 24" (1780 x 610mm) for this example	1
Ⓓ Hinges for the lid			2
Nails or screws			

Consider placing your cold frame next to a building; this will help trap heat around the structure at night.

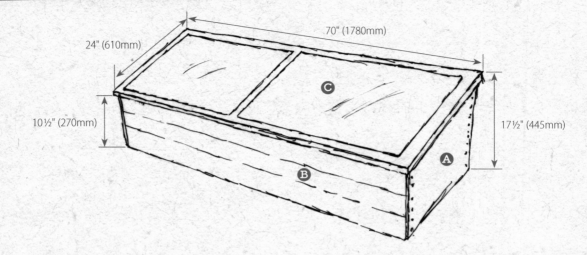

24" (610mm)

70" (1780mm)

C

10½" (270mm)

17½" (445mm)

B

A

1 Cut out the end panels. You can build cold frames in any size or configuration you'd like: I usually have a couple of old windows around that determine the cold frame size I end up with. In this case, I had an old glass window that measured 70" x 24" (1780 x 610mm). I cut out a pair of end panels (A) from some scrap plywood in a size and shape that worked, with a 24" (610mm)-deep top set at an angle. You want about a 25° angle— just eyeball it. A jigsaw or circular saw would both be good tools to cut out the panels.

2 Construct the front and back. Since I had a pile of old 2x4s to work with, that is what I used for the front and back (B) of the cold frame. You could also use ¾" (17mm) plywood for this. Working on sawhorses made it easier than having the parts sit directly on the ground.

1

2

3 **Rip the top back 2x4.** The top 2x4 on the back of the frame needed to be ripped at an angle to accommodate the sloping glass top. I didn't bother to measure this angle precisely: I just traced the edge of the plywood end panel (A) onto the end of the 2x4. With the 2x4 placed flat on my table saw, I adjusted the blade angle until it matched the line I had scribed. Because this isn't precise, furniture-grade work, knowing the exact measurement of the angle isn't particularly important. Close enough is just fine. The photo above right shows the finished intersection between the end panel and the top 2x4 that was ripped at a matching angle.

4 **Install the window.** Get the window (C) in place. An inexpensive pair of hinges (D) will make it easy to open the lid.

Place your cold frame in a section of your garden that has a slight slope to ensure proper drainage.

WIRE MESH CLOCHE
Sturdy Cloche Will Protect Your Plants From Frost

A cloche is a simple structure, usually 2 or 3 feet (610–915mm) high, used to protect a cluster or row of plants from inclement weather. It also functions to keep in the heat of the sun, thus raising the air temperature and allowing plants to flourish when they might otherwise struggle to survive. Cloches are not generally necessary during the main growing season, but they're a great way to start growing earlier in the spring and to extend the season later into the fall. You might even be able to use a cloche to grow plants throughout the winter months.

The cloche described here is one of my favorite designs due to its simplicity and versatility. It uses 4´x 7´ (1220 x 2135mm) sheets of wire mesh designed to reinforce concrete. This material adapts well to this new use because it is made of really thick wire that holds its shape without distorting when bent into a curve. I experimented with different types of wire fencing materials, but this is the only material I've found to be rigid enough to really hold up in the long term. This project describes the process for building a 4´ x 4´ (1220 x 1220mm) cloche, but you could easily build larger frames using 8´ (2440mm) or even 12´ (3660mm) 2x4s, and then use two or three sheets of wire

mesh to create a longer cloche. You could also just build a few of these smaller units and line them up end-to-end as needed. You also have some latitude in how you handle the ends: it is not uncommon for people to just let the plastic overhang the ends and then tuck it in underneath the wooden frame, or you could build more elaborate end caps from plywood.

In terms of the plastic you use to cover the frame, I suggest shopping around to find the material that best suits your needs. Most garden centers will sell varying grades of polyethylene, and they differ in thickness, which determines the number of years that they're expected to last. You can also apply two layers to add extra insulation.

WIRE MESH CLOCHE MATERIALS LIST

item	materials	dimensions	qty.
A Frame	2x2 (38 x 38mm)	48" (1220mm)	4
B Film support	Concrete reinforcing wire mesh	48" x 84" (1220 x 2135mm)	1
C Outside layer	Greenhouse film	8'x10' (2440 x 3050mm)	1
D Scrap wood strips	2x2 (38 x 38mm) (note this dimension isn't critical)	44" (1120mm)	2
E Door	½" (11mm) plywood	48" x 36" (1220 x 915mm)	1
⅝" (15mm) staples			
Nails or screws			

Cloche is a French word meaning "bell," like the ones rung in churches.

PVC CLOCHE
Lightweight PVC Makes This Project A Snap

This style of cloche is pretty common in our area, and for good reason: they're simple, inexpensive, and versatile. You can adapt them to fit just about any size area you'd like, and with a little imagination, you can even scale it up and build a large walk-in hoop house. I do recommend doing this with a partner if you can, because the long lengths of PVC tubing can be frustrating to try and handle on your own.

I used ½" (13mm)-diameter PVC tubing and standard T connectors from the plumbing section of our local home center, and that aspect of the construction is pretty self-explanatory. The 10' (3050mm)-long tubes easily bend to create a cloche that is 8' (2440mm) wide and about 3' (915mm) high, but you could bend them to a tighter radius, which would produce an arch that is narrower and taller. You could also cut the tubes down—when in doubt, I suggest buying one or two extra lengths and experimenting to figure out the size that will work best for you.

PVC CLOCHE MATERIALS LIST

item		materials	dimensions	qty.
A	Base	½" (13mm)-diameter PVC tubing	30" (760mm)	4
B	Ribs	½" (13mm)-diameter PVC tubing	10' (3050mm)	3
C	Connectors	½" (13mm)-diameter T fittings		6 (or you could use 4 right-angles for the ends)
D	Nylon string		8' (2440mm)	3
E	Plastic covering	Greenhouse film	11' x 11' (3355 x 3355mm)	1
F	PVC Clips	¾" (19mm)-diameter tubing	3" (75mm) (Cut in half)	10 total, so 5 lengths of tubing that are then cut in half
G	End clips	Office supply binder clips	Any size will work	4

 Remember, the seeds for your winter garden must be in the ground by mid-summer or early fall.

OPEN SEASON
growing season extenders

137

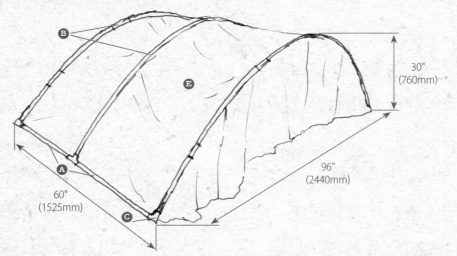

B

E

30"
(760mm)

96"
(2440mm)

A

60"
(1525mm)

C

1 **Prepare the ribs and base.**
I cut up the base tubing (A) into 30"
(760mm) lengths, so you can see
this project will be 60" (1525mm)
long (well, slightly longer, since each
connector adds an inch [25mm] or so).
Lay out the base pieces (A), rib pieces
(B), and T connectors (C) as shown. The
T connectors (C) make it easy to join
the sections of tubing (A, B). I didn't
use any glue, since it is nice to be able
to break down a cloche and store the
parts when it isn't needed, but you
might want to use glue if you plan on
building a more permanent structure.
You could join as many sections
together as you'd like.

2 **Bend the cloche.** To spring the flat
assembly into shape, I tied some nylon
twine (D) on one side and then pulled
it taut and tied it off on the opposing
side. I placed a length of string below
each PVC rib (B), and this worked great.
The finished skeleton is extremely
lightweight and easy to move around.
Having an assistant would've made this
step a lot easier, though.

3 Create clips. To hold the plastic to the frame, I made a set of clips (F) using ¾" (20mm) PVC. I used my table saw to make two parallel rip cuts, thus removing a portion of the center of the tubing. Viewed from the end, the tubing was shaped like a C instead of an O. I then cut the tubing into 3" (75mm) chunks on my chop saw. I suggest making a pile of the clips, since it is better to have too many than too few. You can also buy these clips from most garden supply centers for around 50 cents a piece. If you have a table saw, this method will save you a few bucks—the homemade version will cost about 10 cents each.

4 Attach plastic. The finished clips (F) just click onto the skeleton base (A) and hold the plastic (E) in place. Put two or three on each base piece (A). To attach the plastic (E) to the nylon twine (D) on the ends, simply fold the plastic under the twine and secure with a binder clip (G).

Cloches were originally used primarily in England and continue to be a favorite tool of UK gardeners.

CREATURE COMFORTS
Dwellings for Your Backyard Friends

After you've mastered the art of planting and harvesting vegetables and fruits, you may wish for a greater challenge on your backyard farm. For those of you wanting to delve further into the farming venture, there are some good animals to start with. Bees and rabbits are relatively simple, but definitely each have their own challenges—but building homes for them is easy, at least!

KEVIN & CELIA

Poster Children for Backyard Farming
Salt Lake City, Utah

Kevin and Celia are an amazing couple who are poster children for what is possible if you have the vision and the drive to produce food on your own property. They have a half-acre (2025 square meter) lot—quite large by city standards—where they raise a large variety of crops and animals. Setting foot onto their homestead will definitely make you stop and think; their story is both colorful and inspiring.

Both Salt Lake natives (although Kevin spent the early portion of his childhood in California), Kevin and Celia have been married for 16 years. After graduating from college, they found themselves looking over their options, and they decided to try out life on a commune. This desire led them to spend three years at East Wind Community in rural Missouri. Celia says this is where she learned her gardening and homesteading skills. She's been at it full-time for fourteen years now, and even though we didn't discuss the number of hours she puts in on a weekly basis, I'm guessing it is more than the forty hours of work a week most of us are used to. Kevin works full-time as the GIS Coordinator for Salt Lake City, and his time at home is also used to tend to their crops and animals.

preparing the homestead

When they returned to Salt Lake and moved into the property they now call home, they had a tremendous amount of work to do: the site had formerly been used as an automotive paint shop, and had a large gravel driveway that looped across the yard. Not one to shy away from hard work, Kevin promptly rented a Bobcat and proceeded to clear that portion of the lot and prepare it for planting. This meant doing a ton of work to improve the soil: they had two large dumptrucks full of dead leaves delivered, and Kevin recalls that they were piled almost three and a half feet (1000mm) high. To grind them up, he walked back and forth through the piles while carrying a running lawnmower, thereby shredding the leaves to a size that could be plowed into the ground. This anecdote paints a great picture of Kevin's tenacity and dedication—I used to think I was a tough guy, but not anymore!

↑ How much food can you grow on a half acre? Just ask Kevin and Celia.

Before you buy chickens, decide if you want to raise them for eggs, meat, or both. Then, select a breed suited to your wishes.

Anyway, this extreme method seems to have worked out great, and it makes for a heck of a story, but it did mark the unfortunate beginning of what would become ongoing difficulties with a next-door neighbor who has objected to many of their projects since. Despite their own willingness to get along, this neighbor has not made things easy for them. They fortunately have great relationships with many other folks in their area, and are lucky to count the people at Wasatch Co-Housing (a cluster of over 30 residences) as good neighbors. Their neighborhood is full of gardens and woods and trails, and it doesn't seem possible that such a peaceful, quiet spot is right smack in the middle of a large city.

keeping critters

Kevin and Celia have a broad range of things growing on their land: in addition to dozens of varieties of vegetables, herbs, and fruit, they keep bees, chickens, and goats.

BEES

Their bees are housed in both top bar and conventional hives. Celia noted that the bees can be tricky to work with—there are a lot of things that can go wrong and endanger the health of a colony, and it can be tough to know exactly what is going on.

CHICKENS

They also designed a spacious coop for their fifteen chickens. It is Kevin and Celia's second coop, so they had a lot of

⬆ The bees are housed in both conventional and top bar hives.

⬅ The chickens have a ton of room in which to forage and putter around.

experience to draw from when they set about to build it. The coop is tall enough for them to walk into comfortably, which makes chores easier, and the nesting boxes are far enough out of the way to keep the chickens from tracking manure onto the eggs. The interior of the coop features a set of trays below the roost where the

➜ The interior of the chicken coop is roomy enough for people to enter and move around comfortably, which is handy.

➜ The goat barn is beautiful and functional—a neat DIY accomplishment.

GOATS

Kevin and Celia's latest venture is raising goats, which they've been at for about a year and a half. It sounds like it has been a lot of work—there is naturally a big learning curve to an ambitious project like this—although it does have its rewards. Celia stressed the importance of having a good vet you have confidence in—sound advice, for sure. Their goats are a mixed breed with Saanen, Angora, and Alpine heritage. The goats are very friendly and seem quite at home in their very roomy quarters. The goat barn is a sturdy structure that Kevin and Celia built off of the side of the garage, and it features a nifty system of runs that can be opened up and closed off as needed. Celia remarked that this was handy during birthing season so animals can be isolated yet still all have access to the outdoors. They have plans for a huge new barn built with traditional timber-frame style construction. It will be tall, probably three stories, with a hayloft and plenty of room for both animals and storage.

For milking, there is a simple wooden platform about two feet (600mm) high with a stanchion to ensure that the goat stays put. Celia does the milking by hand, as it is more efficient than setting up and maintaining milking machines when you're not milking a lot of animals. I grew up on a dairy farm, and can attest to this: you would spend an awful lot of time just cleaning and prepping equipment,

chicken droppings are collected. These trays can be removed from the outside and emptied directly into a wheelbarrow. It is the kind of thing that makes perfect sense, but that you would probably only think of if you had done things the hard way for a while first.

Did you know that goats have square pupils? Take a close look the next time you see one!

and a small operation is better off just cutting out this added labor. As it is, Celia already has to be up before the sun for milking every day, so the days are already long enough without making things unnecessarily complicated.

making cheese

One of the best parts about having goats, at least from my point of view, would have to be the easy access to quality milk for making cheese. I've always wanted to dabble in cheese making, and I was lucky enough to get to watch Celia make a batch of chevre. Her demeanor as she worked was casual yet focused, in the way of someone who is very experienced, and I was hooked when I got to taste some. (In fact, I ordered my first cheese making kit as soon as I got home!) Celia commented that cheese making is definitely the area where the goats start to pay their way, because they need to be fed and cared

↑ The interior of the barn is cozy and dry. It can be opened up easily in the summer to keep the temperature down, and it can be buttoned up in the winter to keep the goats warm.

↑ The goats are milked the old fashioned way—no need for machines on a small scale venture like this one. Doing things by hand is faster, easier, and less expensive.

↑ The goat milking platform is set up just a few steps from their back door; a good plan since Celia is out there twice a day, every day.

⬆ Watching Celia make cheese was a real highlight. This milk was only minutes old when she began the process of turning it into chevre.

for a while before they are able to be milked. She gets about half a gallon (2 liters) of milk per goat per day, and this quickly adds up to make some impressive quantities of delicious cheese.

Although they have sold their produce in the past, and Kevin's brother owns a popular local CSA, their present efforts are really geared toward producing food for their own consumption. Celia and I chatted about the challenges inherent in trying to make a living selling home-grown produce—it is certainly not an easy business to be in—and I don't blame them for keeping things simple and focusing on feeding themselves first and foremost. In doing so, they are providing terrific examples to the ever-growing contingent of like-minded people around them—I know that I've learned a lot from them already, and I'm proud to have them as part of my community. They're also a perfect embodiment of the DIY spirit that this book is all about.

LEGAL ISSUES

Before you jump in and get yourself some goats, you'll want to make sure that you're on the right side of the law, particularly if you live in an urban area. Some properties in our city, for example, have animal rights attached to their titles and are thus grandfathered in, as long as they aren't constrained by newer ordinances. Just be sure to do your homework—in this day and age, you can probably just check online at your municipality's Web site.

If it's your first time making cheese at home, try an easy process like cottage cheese before trying more complex cheeses.

TOP BAR BEE HIVE
Easy-to-Use and Maintain Hive Style

As the last few years have seen great losses in the number of bees in nature, beekeeping is a pastime that desperately needs some promotion. The local and global implications of smaller bee populations are urgent: most crops require bees for pollination if they are to bear fruit, and this has a direct effect on the price and availability of food, as well as the overall health of ecosystems. With factors such as these in mind—not to mention having a robust source for delicious honey right outside your door—backyard beekeeping is looking better and better all the time. Please note that this section isn't intended as a comprehensive resource, but taken in conjunction with other educational materials, I think it provides a novel and exciting look into a simple approach to beekeeping.

The style of hives most laypeople are familiar with are Langstroth or National hives. These are stackable units that are built, over the course of a season, into small towers as the hive grows. These hives can be built by anybody who is handy and has access to some basic tools, but they are also available in kit form from numerous retailers both online and in brick-and-mortar stores all over the country. If you purchase them unassembled, they are quite economical. In fact, building them from scratch is generally a worse value proposition when you consider the cost of the raw materials and the time you'll invest in construction. For this reason, I wanted to present a functional design that could actually be built for less money than the standard hives as an alternative for budget-conscious farmers.

The top bar hive is a very old design, dating back probably several thousand years. As it is perhaps the earliest known method for keeping bees, it is quite simple: a long wooden box is fitted with a series of removable bars near its top, and the bees build their honeycombs on the underside of the bars. The box requires a removable top and a single entrance with a small landing platform on one end. The entire assembly is usually raised up on four legs. This means that the hive is positioned at a height that is easy to work at, and there is no heavy lifting involved as would be the case with other types of hives. An open, screened bottom provides ventilation. In terms of capacity, a top bar hive is roughly equivalent to a National hive stacked three boxes deep, so there is plenty of space for a great harvest of both honey

Bees must collect pollen from 2 million flowers to produce one pound (454g) of honey.

and wax. Also, the overall functioning of the hive couldn't be simpler: just remove honeycombs periodically throughout the year when they're surplus to the needs of the colony.

This design features a Plexiglass window on the side, which is not only a neat way of showing off to visitors, but more importantly, has the obvious practical value of allowing the beekeeper to inspect the interior of the hive without disturbing it. When bees are disturbed too frequently, they can become stressed, and this can affect the overall health of the colony.

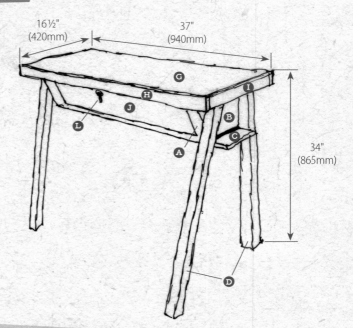

TOP BAR BEE HIVE MATERIALS LIST

item	materials	dimensions	quantity
A Sides	1x8 (19 x 190mm)	34" (865mm)	2
B End caps	1x8 (19 x 190mm)	14" (355mm)	2
C Bottom panel	⅜" (8mm) plywood	37" x 8¼" (940 x 210mm)	1
D Legs	2x2 (38 x 38mm)	36" (915mm)	4
E Viewing window	Plexiglas	29" x 6½" (740 x 165mm)	1
F Grooved bars	Hardwood	1¼" x ¾" x 15¼" (30 x 20 x 390mm)	26
G Top panel	¼" (6mm) plywood	37" x 18" (940 x 460mm)	1
H Top frame long sides	Hardwood	1¼" x ¾" x 37" (30 x 20 x 940mm)	2
I Top frame short sides		1¼" x ⅜" x 16½" (30 x 10 x 420mm)	2
J Window cover	⅜" (8mm) plywood	30" x 7" (760 x 180mm)	1
K Window cover hardware	T-nut	To fit part L	1 each
L Window cover handle	Knob or lever	Any size	1 each
Nails or screws			
Silicone caulk			
Glue			

1 Cut the sides and end caps. As I researched top bar beekeeping, I was continually struck by how simple the hives are. I began by getting a pair of 48" (1220mm) long 1x8 (19 x 190mm) boards. I cut 14" (355mm) from the end of each board—the offcuts would be used as end caps (B) for the hive, while the two longer sections would become the sides (A). The great thing about this design is that you aren't limited to any exact dimensions, so if you have some material on hand that varies slightly, just go ahead and use it.

2 Angle the end caps. The end caps (B) need to be cut at an angle, and a chop saw is a good tool for this. I stacked the parts on top of each other to speed up the process.

3 Thin the end caps. To fit neatly against the sides, I removed about ½" (13mm) from the top of each end cap (B). Not doing this would mean that the end caps would protrude above the sides (A), which are effectively shorter because they are placed at an angle. I also cut ⅜" (10mm) from the bottom of one of the end caps. This creates a small gap between the end cap and the bottom of the hive to serve as an entrance for the bees.

Honeybees communicate with one another by "dancing," performing a series of movements that can be interpreted by other bees.

4

5

4 Create a hole in one side. One of the sides (A) will get a Plexiglas viewing window (E). I decided that the simplest way to do this was to just cut out a hole in one of the boards (A). The other option would have been to build this side from smaller parts. I used a jigsaw to make the cutout.

5 Assemble the sides and end caps. I used a nail gun to assemble the body of the hive, but you could use screws too. I found the easiest way was to assemble the hive upside down on a pair of sawhorses.

6 Attach the bottom. The bottom of the hive is just a piece of ⅜" (10mm) plywood (C) that measures 3" (75mm) longer than the overall length of the hive itself. The extra length should be left to hang over on the side that has the entrance (remember the cut made in Step 3?)—it will serve as a landing platform for the bees as they come in and out of the hive. Use nails or screws to attach the bottom (C).

6

7 Cut and attach the legs. This design is unique for many reasons, one of which is the fact that it sits up off the ground on a set of legs (D). The legs are just 2x2 (38 x 38mm) lumber cut at a 15° angle on their tops. The angle is cut so the tops of the legs will be flat with the tops of the end caps, while the legs themselves are at a sturdy angle. I used a nail gun to tack them onto the hive body, and then used screws from the inside of the hive to beef up the joint between the body and the legs.

7

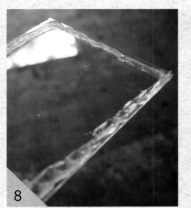

8

9

10

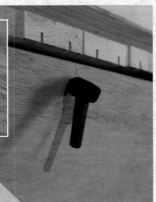

11

8 Attach the viewing window. The Plexiglas window (E) was secured with a bead of silicone caulk. I set it on the inside of the cutout (A), as I knew that I would later fashion a cover for the window (J) and that the cover would go on the outside.

9 Make the grooved bars. The heart of this system is a set of bars (F) that hang across the open cavity of the hive body. The bees will cling to the bottom of these bars and build comb there. The bars are easily removable for when you need to inspect the hive up close or harvest the honey. I cut a ⁵⁄₁₆" (8mm)-wide groove in the bottom of each bar—this is to give the bees a place to cling to and attach the honeycomb.

10 Make the top. The top is a simple shallow box (seen upside down in this photo) consisting of a hardwood frame (H, I) and a thin plywood top (G). The top will need to be weatherproofed in some fashion—covering it with tin would be ideal. The actual construction of the top is pretty straightforward. Nail through the plywood piece (G) into the short (I) and long (H) frame sides— and don't forget the glue.

11 Make the window cover. To fasten the cover of the window (J) to the hive body, I used a T-nut (K) and a small threaded lever (L). A threaded knob would be great, too, but this was what I had on hand, so I went with it. The T-nut went into a hole that I drilled in the side panel, and the lever was threaded into the T-nut.

Each bee colony has a specific odor so bees can distinguish their hive from another.

RABBIT HUTCH
Easy-to-Move Shelf-Style Hutch

I have a three-year-old daughter, and that's why I have a rabbit. At least, that's how it looks at first glance. Take a peek behind the scenes, however, and you'll find out one of my favorite gardening secrets: there's nothing like rabbit manure to rejuvenate tired gardening soil. It has all the advantages of horse manure, with the added benefit of being ready to use immediately without needing to be aged first. It won't burn plants or cause any other problems, as rabbits are herbivores and their waste is pretty tame.

Rabbit manure is a first-rate fertilizer, soil conditioner, and compost ingredient. I actually add it directly to our garden beds, although a lot of people cycle it through their compost piles first. Our plants have always responded well to it, and I'm all for keeping things simple when I can. One of the great things about rabbit manure is how quickly it piles up: we only have one rabbit, but boy does he produce a lot of droppings! This seemed like a headache until my wife started putting it on the gardens, and we began to see that we had a great little asset on our hands. And, occasionally, in our hands, for petting purposes.

Rabbit hutches are simple to build— rabbits mostly need a dry place that is sheltered from wind and snow in the winter and excessive heat in the summer. With that in mind, we actually move ours seasonally, so we place a fairly high value on making our hutch lightweight. Hutches need some kind of roofing that will stand up to the elements—we used old recycled corrugated tin panels. The overall design, in terms of size and aesthetics, is flexible.

A rabbit can see behind itself; its only true blind spot is right in front of its face.

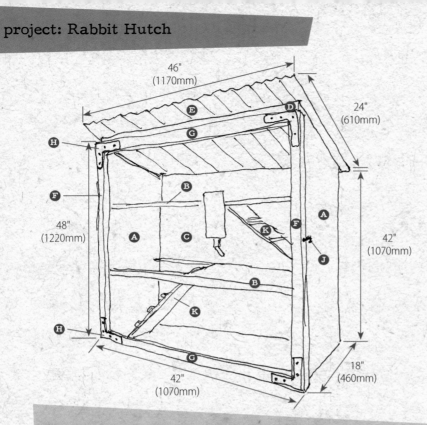

RABBIT HUTCH MATERIALS LIST

	item	materials	dimensions	quantity
A	Side panels	¾" (17mm) plywood	48" x 18" (1220 x 460mm)	2
B	Floor panels	¾" (17mm) plywood	40½" x 18" (1030 x 460mm)	2
C	Back panel	¾" (17mm) plywood	42" x 42" (1070 x 1070mm)	1
D	Top rail	1x3 (19 x 63mm)	40½" (1030mm)	1
E	Roof	Galvanized roof panel	46" x 24" (1170 x 610mm)	1
F	Door stiles	2x2 (38 x 38mm)	41½" (1055mm)	2
G	Door rails	2x2 (38 x 38mm)	39" (990mm)	2
H	Door joiners	Galvanized L brackets	Any size	4
I	Door covering	Chicken wire	42" x 42" (1070 x 1070mm)	1
J	Door hinges	Eye hooks	Any size	2
K	Ramps	Scrap wood and plywood		
	Nails and screws			
	Galvanized roof fasteners			
	Staples			

1 Cut the sides and floor panels.
I fabricated this rabbit hutch out of ¾" (17mm) plywood. I cut out two identical side panels (A) that tapered to create a sloped roof, and made two floors (B) that fit in sort of like the shelves on a bookcase. Come to think of it, my furniture-making background may have subconsciously influenced this design. This hutch is pretty much a bookcase to hold bunnies, not books. The easiest way to assemble something like this is face down on the floor (the project, not the person doing the assembling). I used a nail gun to hold the parts together (this step meant that I didn't need to use clamps, which works well, and it is a nice time-saver). To reinforce the connections, I used 2½" (65mm) screws.

2 Attach the back panel. A unit like this gets most of its strength from the back panel (C). It keeps the whole thing from racking (swaying side-to-side). I also suggest placing screws through the back into the horizontal parts, too.

3 Create and install the top rail.
The hutch needs a rail (D) across the top so that there is a good place to secure the roof panels (E). I angled the blade on my table saw and ripped this 1x3 (19 x 63mm) to follow the slope of the side panel (A).

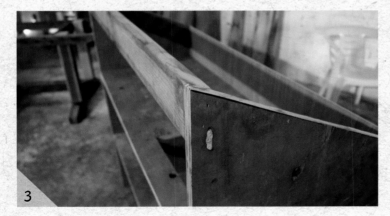

A rabbit can jump as high as 36" (900mm), sometimes higher.

4 Attach the roofing. I screwed the roofing (E) down at 3" (75mm) intervals, and I made sure to use special fasteners made for this purpose. They're like regular screws, except they have a hex-drive head and are fitted with a rubber washer that compresses to seal the holes and prevent leaks.

5 Make the door frame. I made the door from 2x2s (F, G), and joined the horizontal and vertical components with simple L brackets (H). They're galvanized, so they'll last outdoors, and they should help to keep the door in one piece for a long time to come.

6 Complete the door. I covered the entire span of the door with a thick wire mesh (I), which I stapled down. I recommend placing a staple every 3" (75mm) or so. This door is attached with two eye hooks (J). There is one on each side, which means you can open one of them and the door will function almost as if it is on hinges. This was an experiment in seeing how simple I could keep things: it seems to work just fine. I made a couple ramps (K) out of scrap plywood so the rabbit can get from floor to floor (B). Nail some skinny scrap wood across the ramp to help with traction.

4

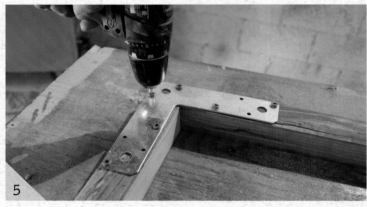

5

6

INDEX

ACQUISITION EDITOR
Peg Couch

ASSISTANT EDITOR
Katie Weeber

COPY EDITOR
Paul Hambke

COVER AND INTERIOR DESIGN
Lindsay Hess

DEVELOPMENTAL EDITOR
Kerri Landis

PAGE LAYOUT
Maura J. Zimmer

PROOFREADER
Lynda Jo Runkle

More Great Books from Fox Chapel Publishing

Art of the Chicken Coop
A Fun and Essential Guide to Housing Your Peeps
By Chris Gleason

A fresh approach to designing and building chicken coops with seven stylish designs that your flock will adore and your neighbors will envy.

ISBN: 978-1-56523-542-7
$19.95 • 160 Pages

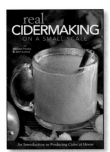

Real Cidermaking on a Small Scale
An Introduction to Producing Cider at Home
By Michael Pooley & John Lomax

Learn everything you need to know about the process of making hard cider from any kind of apple in your home.

ISBN: 978-1-56523-604-2
$12.95 • 112 Pages

The Beekeeping Handbook
A Practical Apiary Guide for the Yard, Garden, and Rooftop
By Vivian Head

Provides the backyard farmer and honey artisan with all the fundamental knowledge needed to take the sting out of beekeeping.

ISBN: 978-1-56523-681-3
$12.95 • 160 Pages

With these little books in hand, you'll be able to impress your friends by identifying any beast you happen to encounter, almost anywhere in the world.

Know Your Pigs
ISBN: 978-1-56523-611-0
$6.95 • 64 Pages

Know Your Donkeys & Mules
ISBN: 978-1-56523-614-1
$6.95 • 80 Pages

Know Your Chickens
ISBN: 978-1-56523-612-7
$6.95 • 96 pages

Know Your Cows
ISBN: 978-1-56523-613-4
$6.95 • 96 pages

You Bet Your Garden Guide to Growing Great Tomatoes
How to Grow Great-Tasting Tomatoes in Any Backyard, Garden, or Container
By Mike McGrath

From backyards to terraces, this deliciously funny little book is also a serious guide on how to start and nurture an heirloom tomato patch.

ISBN: 978-1-56523-710-0
$14.95 • 112 Pages

Look for These Books at Your Local Bookstore or Specialty Retailer
To order direct, call **800-457-9112** or visit *www.FoxChapelPublishing.com*
By mail, please send check or money order + S&H to:
Fox Chapel Publishing, 1970 Broad Street, East Petersburg, PA 17520

VISA	# Item	US Shipping Rate
Master Card	1 Item	$3.99
	Each Additional	.99

Canadian & International Orders – please email info@foxchapelpublishing.co